Berthold Schmutzhart is the Chairman of Sculpture at the Corcoran School of Art, Washington, D.C. He also teaches a furniture design and construction class at the Smithsonian Institution, Washington, D.C. He is an award-winning artist whose work has been featured in exhibits throughout the United States.

THE HANDMADE FURNITURE BOOK

Berthold Schmutzhart

PRENTICE-HALL, INC. Englewood Cliffs, N.J. 07632

A SPECTRUM BOOK

Library of Congress Cataloging in Publication Data

Schmutzhart, Berthold.
    The handmade furniture book.

    (A Spectrum Book)
    Bibliography: p.
    1. Furniture making—Amateurs' manuals.   I. Title.
TT195.S34   684.1'042   81-1867
ISBN   0-13-383638-X   AACR2
ISBN   0-13-383620-7 (pbk.)

This Spectrum Book can be made available to businesses and organizations at a special discount when ordered in large quantities. For more information contact: Prentice-Hall, Inc., General Book Marketing, Special Sales Division, Englewood Cliffs, New Jersey 07632

Editorial/production supervision and interior design by Cyndy Lyle
Manufacturing buyer Barbara Frick
Art production by Marie Alexander
Interior photographs by Richard Conroy and Simin Hassanzadeh
Interior illustrations by Bruce Gibson

Prentice-Hall International, Inc., *London*
Prentice-Hall of Australia Pty. Limited, *Sydney*
Prentice-Hall of Canada, Ltd., *Toronto*
Prentice-Hall of India Private Limited, *New Delhi*
Prentice-Hall of Japan, Inc., *Tokyo*
Prentice-Hall of Southeast Asia, Pte. Ltd., *Singapore*
Whitehall Books Limited, *Wellington, New Zealand*

Contents

Foreword

The first time I heard about Bert Schmutzhart, he was working on a sculpture commission for a church. The Christ figure was so long Bert had to work on it with the head sticking out of his front door and the feet out the back door.

The next time was when the students at the Corcoran School of Art rose as a single body to defend Bert against another teacher who thought that Bert taught the techniques of sculpture too well. The other teacher was unhappy because Bert's students learned how to use a hammer and chisel before going to to manipulate laser beams.

I have other favorite Bert stories. When he was remodeling a house on Capital Hill, he had almost finished the inside when the rains came and opened a watercourse in the roof. Bert, with no chance to fix the roof in the storm, installed a drain pipe over the drip and piped the water outside.

We watched him build his glider for years and trembled when he gave an art critic a ride. He put the finishing touches on it in our yard, and it was like having a great outdoor sculpture.

We live with two of Bert's best sculptures in our front hall—one of his "dream swimmers," carved out of a hunk of wood, and one of his "anchovy cans with ducks" made of steel and wood. Our visitors marvel.

But Bert has never been so preoccupied with his own work as a sculptor that he hasn't had time to teach others. Students on two continents have agreed that as a teacher he is a genius. His ability to reach out to students is legendary.

In his native Austria, he worked out a way to make friends with refugee children by learning their own folkways. In Washington he taught sculpture to a blind child and helped an aphasic child learn to speak out. His work with children who have learning disabilities should have made him a saint like those he restored in several Salzburg churches.

This book is an outgrowth of one of Bert's longest commitments—teaching woodworking at the Smithsonian Associates classes. Bert's classes are always the first to be filled. The universal complaint is that they don't go on forever. And the students in their teacher's report card at the end of the session talk about his humor, his ability to explain, his sincere interest in every student, his patience, and his knowledge.

Bert knows much about tools, wood, design, and art, but most of all about people. I'm very glad he's decided to put a little of it down on paper in this book. And it seems to me his sentences are as neatly dovetailed as his sculpture.

Sarah Booth Conroy

Acknowledgments

We all have teachers. Brilliant teachers, good teachers, and not-so-good teachers come and go. Special teachers, however, stay with us in one way or another.

Two such special people, Tischlermeister Mathias Linzmaier and Tischlermeister Josef Hofer, made a mark in my life. These mastercraftsmen allowed me, for a period of eight years, to look over their shoulders and see how things are done. They patiently replied to my often complicated questions with straightforward and simple answers. I learned during this time that everybody can make a simple thing complicated, but only a few have the insight to make a complicated thing simple. Thank you, Hias and Sepp, you made your point.

I also gratefully acknowledge the personal time, suggestions, critical comments, and other help kindly given by the following people: Richard and Sarah Conroy, Morton Ehudin, Rita Roppolo, Eloise Rosas, Slaithong Schmutzhart, Jane Sylvester, and Peter Thomas.

Introduction

In recent years many new books about furniture and furniture making have appeared and, since this subject is close to my heart, I have read almost all of them.

There are books encompassing the whole history of furniture and others dealing with aspects of it, such as the work of Chippendale or the style of Art Nouveau. The Shakers have had their share of attention, and a very beautiful work has been written about old tools. There is even a book that concentrates solely on New England pine furniture. No end is in sight, and so much the better.

This is not so with technical books about furniture making. First, there are not as many and, second, by no means are they as many-sided. Much more information should be available. The books I have seen deal mostly with industrial woodshops, college programs, and equipment for mass production. This is valid and necessary, but handbuilding single pieces is still a living art.

This book deals with the technical side of handmade furniture, and will, I hope, be useful to you. Today many outstanding, original pieces of furniture are built by one individual for another individual, on one workbench, and quite often with only a few hand-tools, much as they were in the past. There is nothing impractical about this. The fact is, more often than not, it is faster and easier to build one piece by hand than to set up and reset an elaborate machine system normally done for a production line. The few books written about handbuilding seem to miss this point and stress instead a rather romantic note, which in my opinion is out of place.

Cabinetmaking, during thousands of years of practice, has never been anything other than simple, practical, and rational. The book before you will continue in this mode. This is a workbook and should be used as such. To browse through it is not as useful at **working** through it from beginning to end. Each chapter contains important information needed to understand the next chapter. Some questions are not dealt with up front but later on, when a more immediate need to know demands an answer. For instance, the wood chapter really continues throughout the whole book. The same is true for the tool section.

To understand what is being said you must use your hands. There is no other way. Take your tools, a few pieces of wood, and go to it. When you are done, you will have a keen understanding of how furniture is put together and why. Have fun.

Wood 1

Flowering cherry trees
Photo by Bruce Gibson

Wood may well be the most used and versatile material mankind has ever known.

This renewable resource served in the form of a war club at the dawn of human existence. Shaped differently, it became a symbol leading millions into religious ecstasy. Built into ships, it carried countless sailors to every shore of this earth, and made into shelters, it protected us. The first railroad track was laid on it, and in the form of plywood it found its way into space.

In each application an understanding of what wood can and cannot do was needed in order to assure success in its usage. This has not changed. A furniture maker is not exempt from this rule.

A tree, the source of wood, becomes wider and taller every season. Each year a ring, composed of a light band called *earlywood*, grows in the summer. In the winter a dark band develops in the annual ring called *latewood*. The whole growing package is wrapped into three layers known as *cambium*, *inner bark*, and *outer bark*. This cover assures growth and protection. In the center of the tree is the *heartwood*—an accumulation of the annual rings. This darker part is inactive, heavy, strong, and durable. Between the heartwood and the bark is the *sapwood*, which is also comprised of many rings but is lighter in color and weight. The sapwood acts as the food transportation and storage system for the tree, but is an easy target for decay.

This ring system is not the same, in size or appearance, in all trees. There is a wide variety between the different species of trees. In some trees, especially in tropical climates, growth is so continuous that no well-defined annual rings can be seen.

A closer look at wood reveals that it is made of cells that are tightly grown together in a variety of shapes and sizes. The size and shape of the cells directly determines the hardness of the wood, the strength and weight of it, and how well it can be glued. Not least, the beauty of the wood is also influenced by the cells.

All trees are filled with water. Some have a moisture content of 200 percent of their wood substance. Needless to say, once the tree has been cut, the shrinkage and warpage of its wood is a substantial problem. The design of good wooden furniture is directly related to this fact. Even dry wood, with a moisture content of about 7 percent, is not stable. Wood is very sensitive to water, and whenever the humidity of the air changes, wood comes alive and moves. This is the cause of most problems a woodworker has to face.

Luckily, some woods are less unstable than others. This is also true for different cuts of wood. A tree trunk plain-sawed into boards, for instance, produces only one almost stable piece, the centerboard. This board will shrink, but under normal conditions it will not warp as much as all other pieces of this stack. Since this kind of board is most in demand, wood is often cut quarter-sawed to obtain a better yield of stable pieces.

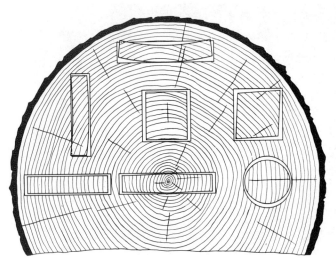

Characteristic shrinkage and distortion of drying wood
Reprinted by permission of the Forest Products Laboratory Forest Service, USDA

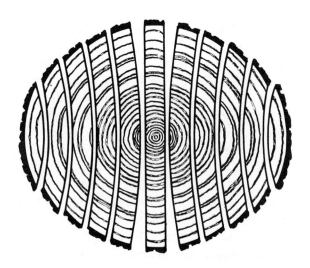

PLAIN SAWED

QUARTER SAWED

If you have ever cut into yellow pine you may have questioned the wisdom of calling it a softwood. Be assured, the label softwood or hardwood has very little to do with the ease with which you can drive a nail into it. The real distinction is that softwoods are needle trees that have their seeds exposed, usually in the form of cones. Hardwoods are trees with broad leaves, and its flowers and seeds are enclosed in a fruit. There are hardwoods much softer than fir or yellow pine.

Closer descriptions of wood are quite often of little help, since the naming and grading of wood is a regional matter. On the West Coast, for example, wood of ladder and pole stock can be purchased. This is clear wood for high-stress use. In the West and Midwest, aircraft-grade spruce is available. This is a tight-grained, straight-grained, and very light wood compared with its strength. In the East you may be asked if you wish to have male or female walnut. The difference is in the amount of heartwood compared with the sapwood of the tree. In areas with wood industries you may have to specify if factory select or select shop is what you need. There is first and second lumber "FAS," common and sound wormy, and so on.

Usually cabinetmakers are more concerned with the beauty of wood than with the grade of it or the loads it can carry. Some understanding, however, about the strength of wood and where it occurs is helpful.

The following comparison, along with a loose structural design sketch for a table using Douglas fir will explain what is involved.

1. Tension parallel to grain—10,900 pounds per square inch
2. Compression parallel to grain—4,420 pounds per square inch
3. Compression perpendicular to grain—1,020 pounds per square inch
4. Shearing stress parallel to grain—950 pounds per square inch
5. Tension perpendicular to grain—140 pounds per square inch

When we compare the tension loads, items 1 and 5, it becomes clear that fir is 77.8 times stronger *with* the grain, than against it. Obviously this will have a strong influence on the design of our imaginary table. Another view is also very informative. From item 2 it is apparent that four legs of fir, each 2 by 2 inches thick, will carry a total load of 67,520 pounds. No need to worry about the legs.

How about the weakest part of such a table? Usually there are tenons holding the legs and the frame of the table together. An effort to answer the above questions can start with the tenons. If we assume that each tenon is 4 inches wide and ½ inch thick, which amounts to a cross section of 2 square inches, we can calculate how strong this element is. We do not have a figure for perpendicular shearing stress. Therefore, 950 pounds per square inch will have to do. One tenon will hold 1,900 pounds. This is not all. Having two tenons in each leg, we deal all together with eight tenons. The result is 15,200 pounds. A strong table, if built right.

Since this is an imaginary table, everything is possible. Let us assume that one piece of the frame is not long enough to make a tenon and a spline has to be made. Would the strength of the table change? No, provided the spline has the same cross section as the replaced tenon and the grain of the spline is aligned with the frame. Since today's glues are stronger than wood there is no need to be concerned about the kind of glue used. There is no question that the strength of this table would not change even if all eight joints between the legs and frames were splined.

One possibility should be considered. If a spline is turned the wrong way—by mistake, of course—and the grain of it should be aligned with the grain of the leg instead of the frame, structural failure becomes a possibility. According to item 4 of our tension comparison for Douglas fir, all would be well were it not for the leg. The leg becomes a lever if pushed sideways, creating tension.

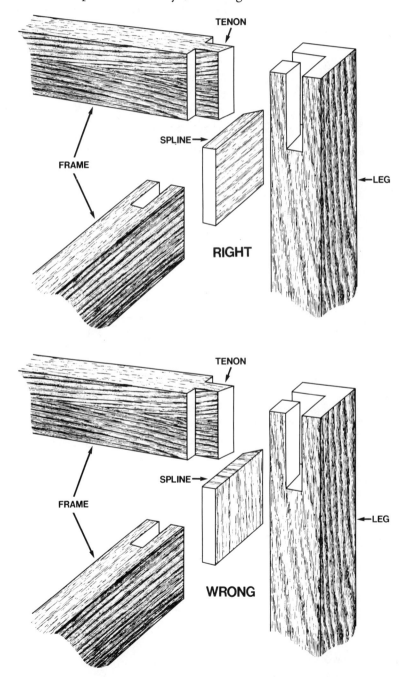

Item 5 tells us what tension can do to a misaligned spline. Remember, we have 2 square inches as a cross section, amounting to a holding power of 280 pounds. We need one other dimension, the length of the leg, to complete our calculation. Assuming the length is 32 inches, the following scenario could unfold:

Somebody pushes or pulls the bottom of the leg with a force of only 9 pounds. This force is multiplied by the length of the lever, 9 by 32, resulting in a moment of 288 inch-pounds. The upper end of the lever, with the spline in it, cannot withstand such force. Needless to say, the joint will break, sending the whole table tumbling down. A child can do it!

There is no need to consider the finer details, such as the column efficiency of the legs or the interacting load factors of the whole structure, before building a piece of furniture. After all, nobody will serve 67,520 pounds of food on one dinner table!

It is more important, for instance, to arrange glue joints in such a way that side grain meets side grain. Glue on end grain does not hold and is useless. *Side grain* is the wood fiber exposed if a tree is split down the midde. *End grain* is exposed on surfaces made by cutting across the trunk of a tree.

The cost of wood and the availability of it is very much a local matter. Local advice and help is needed. A friendly relationship with a person working at the neighborhood lumberyard can be very beneficial. Be aware that almost all woods used for furniture making, hard and soft, are sold as raw materials, rough cut. This means you are expected to pay extra for milling if you wish to have the material planed, cut, and trimmed to meet your needs.

Building lumber, the final product ready for assembly, is usually marketed *dressed*. This means it is cut to standard building sizes, sanded, color-coded, and often treated against dry rot or other diseases.

Off to the lumberyard. Enjoy it!

Tools 2

Old handscrew
Photo by Simin Hassanzadeh

An Austrian story tells that by the end of the Gothic period, around A.D. 1500, cabinetmakers used a device called a *Flammhobel*. This tool produced a wavy, flamelike, three-dimensional surface that was used to decorate the finest of the fine furniture of that time. It was the ultimate plane. Soon after the tool was lost and with it the knowledge of how it worked.

A sad tale. It would be hard to believe were it not that, even in our time, tools come and go. Some tools disappear completely, some get reinvented or rediscovered. Once in a while a perfectly good tool is replaced by an inferior one, and within a few decades the real tool becomes forgotten while the replacement inherits its name. Some saws and planes now in use are living proof of this.

This is not a chapter written to please a tool collector or a lover of antiques. None of the tools were chosen for this purpose. They were selected for their plain, straightforward usefulness in making furniture. Since this book is dedicated to handmade furniture, the tools are hand-held and hand-powered.

If some of the tools you already own are not precisely like the ones shown here, do not be concerned. The appearance is unimportant. A spokeshave with a wooden handle is as good as one with a metal frame. The names of tools are often based on local usage, and there may be two names for the same tool—for example, a try plane and a jointer plane are alike. The key to a fine job is to use the right tool at the right time.

HAMMERS

There must be at least several dozen different hammers, each designed for a special purpose, all of them useful. There are hammers to flatten things, hammers with magnetic tips, hammers for geologists, and, above all, an array of hammers used to join things together using nails.

In making good furniture, nails are used only temporarily in order to keep a joint from slipping. After the nail has served its purpose, it should be removed. For this purpose a claw on the hammer is needed.

Since the rest of the hammer has not changed for centuries, you may as well hold onto your old trusted claw hammer. It will serve you well for the rest of your life.

An inexpensive metal try square can be adjusted to serve as a marking gauge and as a depth gauge, as well as to test for outside and inside square. It also measures 45-degree angles, and it comes with a little scribe attached to it. If you look closely, you will even find a level thrown into the deal. How can you do better? It must be said, however, that unlike several other squares and marking gauges, this tool is not made of rosewood, and lacks elegance. Should you use this square, it would serve you well to have a larger scribe as well.

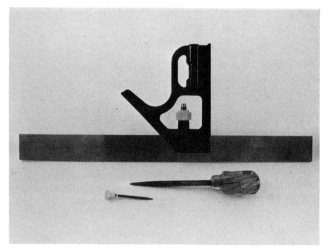

SAWS

If you are the owner of a handsaw, you likely curse a lot. Remember when you first attempted to cut a board across the grain with your freshly sharpened saw? You had to keep lifting the weight of the saw away from the thrust of your cutting. Whenever you relaxed, the saw buried itself into the wood and stopped. It seemed like an endless process. Cutting with the grain took even longer, no matter how hard you pressed down.

Examine your saw and you will find the cause of all your troubles. You have a combination saw, a general-duty tool, invented to save you the expense of purchasing two saws. Needless to say, it does not work very well.

You do need two saws instead of one. First, get a ripsaw, which is designed to cut with the grain of the wood. In this direction all woods are weak, therefore the raked teeth of this tool, meeting barely any resistance, will cut quickly and efficiently.

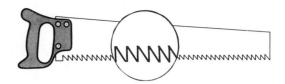

COMBINATION SAW

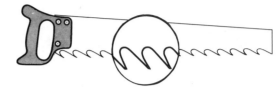

RIP SAW

You also need a crosscut saw. A crosscut saw has to work through many hard fibers and especially through alternating early-wood and latewood rings. To avoid getting hooked in the latewood, the teeth of this saw are straight. This tool is specially designed to cut against the grain. Compared with the ripsaw, which has normally 5 points (points are the number of teeth in an inch), the crosscut saw is much finer—usually 10 points. The crosscut saw in this picture has 14 points.

CROSSCUT SAW

Two specialized saws are true combination saws. They cannot be otherwise, since their use alternates between cutting long and cross-grain. The dovetail saw has a very thin blade of about 18 points and is stiffened on its top. The turning saw also has a combination blade. To enable this saw to cut tight curves, the teeth of the blade are set wide and the height of the blade is only ¼ inch. Both handles holding the blade can be rotated. This saw belongs to the family of frame saws used widely in Europe. This kind of saw comes in all sizes, holding rip and crosscut blades in its frames. The turning saw in the picture has a 9-point blade.

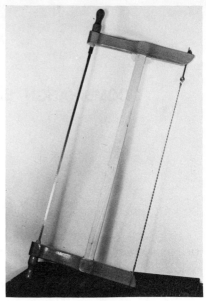

PLANES

Do you have a plane? Take a look at it. It may not be a plane, after all. There is an excellent possibility that you own a scraper instead. In many hardware stores the salesperson does not know the difference between one and the other. A scraper quite often does look like a plane, and the fact that the single blade is arranged upside down does not seem to be important. Well, it is.

All planes have the beveled side of their blades on the bottom and—block planes, rabbet planes, and sometimes scrub planes excepted—they all have a second blade, called the cap iron. There is a good reason for this. The plane blades cut, and by doing so, they lift a thin layer of wood from the surface. Before this thin but stiff layer can pull too much fiber up, the cap iron will break the tension. In addition, the cap iron stabilizes the cutting edge.

All regular planes have the cutting edge of their blades sharpened convex. At no time should the corners of the blade extend beyond the sole of the plane. Only the apex of the cutting edge is used.

The blade of a rabbet plane, or tongue-and-groove plane, is straight. Such planes are designed to cut deep grooves into the material, which necessitates the corners of the cutting edge.

There is not much difference between a wooden or a metal plane. The blades are sharpened the same way, and the tool is certainly used in the same manner. The care for, and adjustment of, the

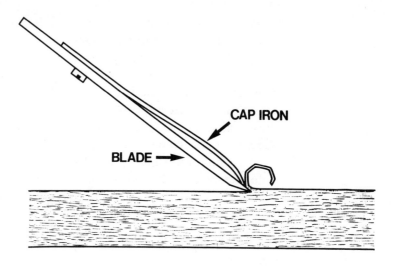

CAP IRON

BLADE →

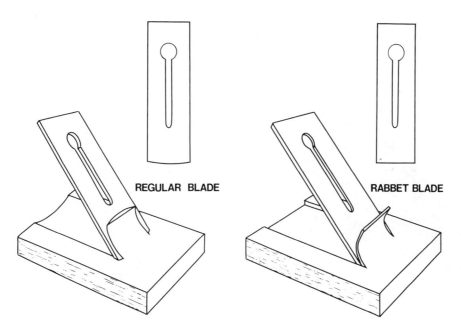

REGULAR BLADE

RABBET BLADE

two tools is slightly different, however. The blade of a metal plane rides on a pin activated by a turning wheel. The pin pushes the blade out or, if needed, returns it closer to the sole of the plane.

A hammer is used to adjust the blade of a wooden plane. The wedge holding the blade in position should sit fairly tight. A light tap with the hammer on the upper end of the blade will push it out. A light tap on the rear of the plane's body will move it back. Do not forget to tighten the wedge after this. To preserve the sole of the wooden plane it is customary to soak it once in a while with hot linseed oil. The following planes are needed to build furniture by hand.

The *scrub plane* pictured may or may not have a double blade, since it is never used to do final work on a surface. The function of this plane is to remove large amounts of uneven wood. This tool is especially useful in preparing rough-sawed surfaces for finer planing. The cutting edge is pronouncedly convex in order to allow the plane to be used against, with, or at an angle to the grain.

The *jointer plane,* also known as a *jack plane* or *try plane* has a double blade. This tool is used to remove the large ridges left by the scrub plane. The long body of this plane is essential in leveling large or long surfaces. The cutting edge is moderately convex. You may cut with this plane up to 45 degrees angular to the grain.

The *smoothing plane* is used to remove the moderate ridges left by the jointer plane. The cutting edge is barely convex, and since the corners of the blade must not touch the material, the bottom of the blade protrudes only a hair from the sole of the plane. The shavings made by a smoothing plane are very thin. Use this tool parallel to the grain only.

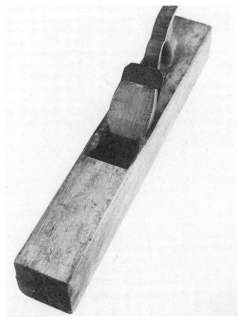

There is only a single blade in a *block plane*. The block plane is used to work the ends of boards; in other words, it is used to cut end grain only. There is no stiff side grain to be pulled up, thus the need for a cap iron does not exist. A small, regular double-bladed plane can cut end grain also.

Since the final surfaces inside a rabbet or a tongue and groove do not have to be pristine, the blades of planes used to cut such shapes are without cap irons. Pictured is a set of *tongue-and-groove planes*.

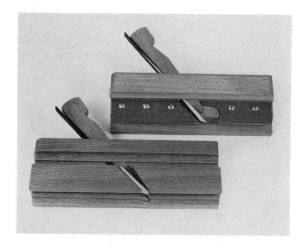

Spokeshave. This very short plane with a handle on each side is used on curved wood. Its blade is arranged to cut, not to scrape.

There is no need for a cap iron, since it is the function of a spokeshave to cut down into the grain of the wood, not parallel to it.

The cabinet scraper is only one version of a wide variety of tools used for the purpose of removing the outer layer of a piece of material. The first scraper may have been a seashell. From early Egyptian times on, sanding stones were widely used as scrapers, ultimately leading to the invention of rasps, files, and sandpaper.

Most scrapers, especially sandpaper, dig into the soft parts of wood, leaving the harder fibers raised, and all scrapers push some of the dust created by scraping into the cells of the wood. This leaves the surfaces ill-prepared for gluing and staining. Glass and steel blades are the cleanest and most efficient of all scrapers.

The cabinet scraper is a blade of tool steel about 2 inches wide and 6 inches long. The thickness is about the same as that of a saw blade.

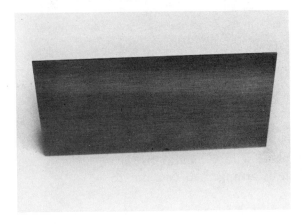

BRACE AND AUGER BITS

Arguments about the relative merits of various drilling devices never seem to end. Each person claims to have the ultimate drill, and more often than not, each claim is correct. The right choice of a drill not only depends on the material to be drilled but where, when, and how the boring is done. A high-speed drill press, as fine a tool as it is, is not in great demand by furniture makers, but a brace with auger bits, as old fashioned as it is, fills all the hand builder's needs.

Augers of all sizes, guided by a screw lead, drill clean holes. The twisted shape of the auger removes the woodshavings, eliminating the need to withdraw the tool every so often for this purpose. The squared shank prevents slippage between auger and brace.

A good brace is equipped with a ratchet. Set into the neutral position, the ratchet allows drilling clockwise into the material and counterclockwise out. The bit, held by the screw lead, cannot be withdrawn except by turning it to the left.

Turned to the extreme right, the ratchet setting locks the bit in the drilling-in position; but it releases its hold when the handle of the brace is moved backward. This ingenious setup enables the user to drill in quarter-turns only, for instance, if needed in a tight corner. When the user wishes to move the bit out, the whole process is reversed by setting the ratchet wheel to the extreme left.

There are wide- and narrow-handled braces, made in several sizes.

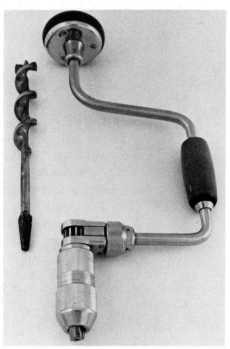

DOWEL CENTERS

The invention of new tools has not come to an end. Dowel centers are living proof of this. If you ever have matched holes for several dowels without this simple tool, you will appreciate progress as soon as you use those aluminum plugs.

The lower end of the dowel center is inserted into one hole of the future dowel joint, with the rim holding it in position. The pin, on top of the plug, marks where the opposite hole should be. Just press the two pieces of a dowel joint together, dowel centers in between, and tap it slightly with a hammer. After separating the pieces, you will see the indentations made by the pins. Drill there and you will have perfectly matched holes for the dowels.

CHISELS

Not all holes in wood are round. To make square holes chisels are needed. For deep or very heavy work mortise chisels with strong, thick blades, compared with ordinary cabinet chisels, are used. For most cabinet work a few common flat chisels, beveled on one side and flat on the other, are quite sufficient.

WOODCARVING CHISELS

If you are a cool, calculating, precise, and orderly person, you must have carving tools made of Sheffield steel. The edges of such chisels, once sharpened, seem to hold forever. But you pay a price for this. If you misuse tools of this sort, the hard but brittle steel will break.

At the other extreme are the Austrian, Swiss, or Italian tools. The steel is softer and much more forgiving. You pay a price for this also: The chisels have to be sharpened more often.

No matter what kind of chisels you choose, they all look and function alike. A flat chisel, chamfered on both sides, a shallow gouge, and a deep gouge are likely to be all the chisels needed to carve whatever you wish. Be certain to match the size of the carving tools with the size of the work you do.

ROUND MALLET

Wear gloves when using this tool the first few times. Most other wooden hammers are made of lighter wood. In order to be effective they are large, which in turn makes them cumbersome. Once you have learned to guide the round mallet without looking at it, however, you will probably dispense with any other wooden hammer you may have.

New mallets are often covered with a layer of wax for protection. It will wear off very fast. To keep the tool from drying out, soak it occasionally with hot linseed oil.

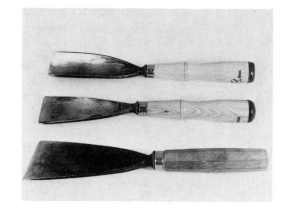

The most important of all tools is a workbench. No matter how luxurious or plain, this tool must meet three requirements.

It must be stable and flat on the top. Decent work cannot be done on a wobbly and uneven bench. If your bench is light, you may have to bolt it to the floor of your shop or find some other way to keep it from sliding.

It must be the right height. The height of a good workbench is related to the height of the user. To measure your workbench, stand up straight in front of it, let your arms hang loose, and form a fist with each hand. Your fists should barely touch the top of your bench. For a 5-foot-6-inch-tall person the right height is about 29 inches. Should the person be taller, the work surface should be raised to meet the fists of this person. For a bench too high, the legs could be shortened. If this is not possible, a small platform for the woodworker to stand on would be a good solution. Height is important to provide the proper leverage for your arms.

It must be possible to fasten all workpieces, vertically and horizontally, to it. Both hands are needed to work. The function of the workbench is to free your hands.

A look at two workbenches—one an absolute minimum bench, the other representing the most desirous—will show how these three requirements are met in each tool.

The first bench is made of common building lumber and is designed to be built in a few hours. The height should be matched to the size of the owner, and the length should not be less than 4 feet. The leg frames, made of 2 × 4's are joined with 1/2-inch dowels. The crosspieces holding the frames together are made of 2 × 6's fastened on each end with a double-bolted butt joint. The bolts of such a joint can be tightened to stabilize the bench legs if necessary.

The work surface, made of two 2 × 10's, is relatively light and must be bolted or screwed on to the frame. It is helpful to countersink whatever fastener is used. The 3-inch gap between the two boards provides space to insert a hand screw for the purpose of holding a horizontally placed workpiece in position. The 2 × 4 inch support under the front edge of the work surface is glued on; it not only strengthens the most-used part of the workbench, it also serves as a place for attaching a hand screw, used to hold a vertical workpiece in position.

This inexpensive but sturdy bench is easy to make and will serve well for a long time.

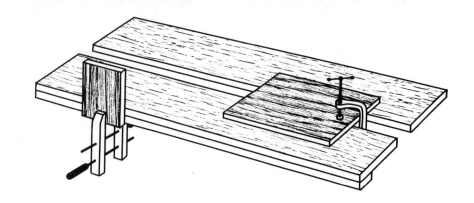

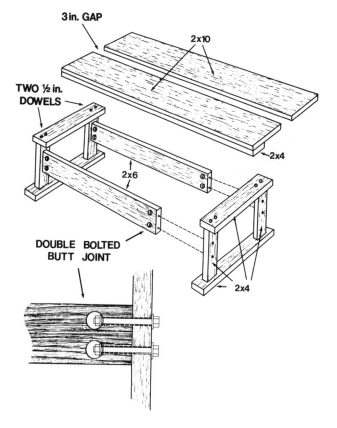

3 in. GAP

2x10

TWO ½ in. DOWELS

2x6

2x4

DOUBLE BOLTED BUTT JOINT

2x4

The second bench is an expensive, factory-produced tool. It is made of fine beechwood or sometimes of white oak. The height must be adjusted if it does not fit the owner. A platform for a short person, or blocks to raise the legs to accommodate a tall person, will do. The bench is made in different lengths. The leg frames are joined with mortises and tenons. The crosspieces holding the frames together are fastened with one long bolt each. This bolt leads from one leg through the length of the crosspiece, and into the other leg; it can be tightened to stabilize the bench legs if necessary.

The work surface is so heavy that gravity alone, helped by a few wooden pins against sliding, hold it in place. The upper front of the work surface has openings to accommodate adjustable metal pins called *benchdogs*. When they are used with the vise on the right, they serve as a long clamp. By placing the left benchdog where needed, long and short horizontal workpieces can be held in place. The left and right vises are designed to hold vertical workpieces in position.

This kind of bench has not changed for centuries. There is no need for improvement.

CLAMPING DEVICES

As with many other tools, clamping devices are made and used in varieties of ways. There are drill press vises, to hold small pieces for better drilling; flooring clamps, to tighten floorboards before nailing them down; corner clamps, used on picture frames; and many others you may need at some time. There are only two kinds of clamps you will use all the time. You need a few wooden hand screws and some bar clamps.

A *hand screw* is a clamping device made of two hardwood blocks connected by two handled screws that allow the blocks to be adjusted to the size and angle of the wood to be glued. After the adjustment is made, a turn of the rear screw tightens the clamp.

A *bar clamp* is usually made of metal and has one fixed and one sliding jaw, both attached to a long bar. After the sliding part of the clamp has been adjusted to the wood to be glued, the vise on the fixed part of the clamp is tightened. This kind of clamp is used on wide and long workpieces.

Hand screws have been with us since the Middle Ages and have changed very little. About 200 years ago, the wooden screws were replaced with metal ones. During the Industrial Revolution the bar clamp as we know it now was introduced. But there are still many places where an old form of this clamp is in use. This tool, made quite easily in any woodshop, consists of two wooden bars with holes to accommodate vertical wooden pins. The pins, inserted wherever needed depending on the width of the workpiece, serve as footholds for wedges. The wedges in turn, tightened with a hammer, exert the pressure needed for gluing. If you use a clamp like this, do not forget to put paper between the clamp and the wood you glue.

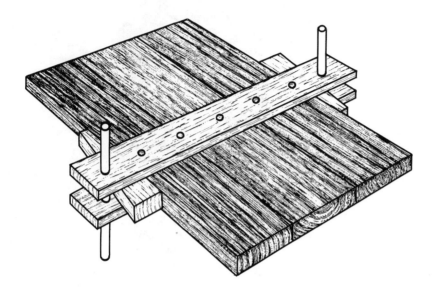

SHARPENING STONES

The sharpening of tools is a craft in itself saddled with elaborate rules and customs. Fortunately the blades of tools used by cabinetmakers are plain and straightforward. There is no need to fret about the cutting angle of a pair of scissors or to worry about the honing of a serrated knife. While some of the woodcarving chisel blades are curved, the basic shape of the cutting edge has not changed. The edge is chamfered and therefore ground from one side only. The sole exception to this is the flat woodcarving chisel.

Let me warn you about the small silicon carbide grinding wheel very much in use today. It is a good grinder, but if you are not very careful, it will burn your tools and thus destroy the temper of the cutting edges. A rule of thumb would state the larger the wheel and the slower it turns, the better it is for your tool. A large, watered sandstone wheel is best.

Most of the sharpening is done on a flat, coarse stone. Take the blade of your tool, chamfered side down, and grind steadily until a burr appears on the upper side of the cutting edge. Do not change the angle of the chamfer.

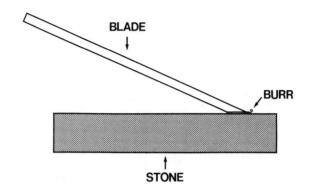

A medium-grit stone is used next. Turn the blade around and grind it until the burr, now a bit smaller, appears on the chamfered side. Keep the blade flat, do not raise it!

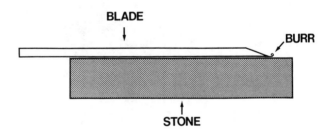

Repeat this procedure many times, ultimately using the finest stone you have. After the burr has fallen off, the blade will be razor sharp.

The sharpening of woodcarving tools is done similarly. When you grind the chamfered side, you should tilt the tool back and forth, allowing the stone to grind all parts of the cutting edge. Work the inside, the flat side, of the tool by holding the chisel steady and moving the stone instead. Keep the stone flat on the chisel, do not raise it! Tear-shaped slipstones of medium and fine grit are used on woodcarving gouges.

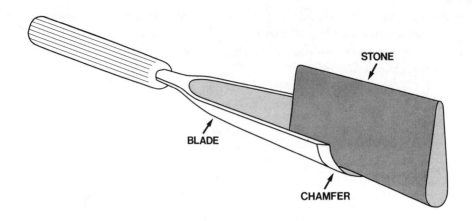

STONE

BLADE

CHAMFER

It does not matter if you use oil- or water-type stones; both are good. Avoid using cooking or linseed oil when sharpening, however; the stones will gum up. If you have done so, boiling them in a pot of water will work wonders. Man-made sharpeners, such as India stones, also known as aluminum oxide stones, will serve well for a long time. Natural stones, Arkansas or Washita, last a lifetime.

Sharpening a Scraper. The cabinet scraper is the only woodworking tool not sharpened with stones. A fine file and the shank of a screwdriver, or any other length of a round toolsteel, is used for this purpose.

To sharpen the scraper, fasten it edge up into a vise or the blocks of a hand screw. Work the file lengthwise on the edge of the scraper to remove nicks and other uneven spots. Then take the handle of the screwdriver into one hand and the business end of it into the other, leaving only a few inches of the shank exposed between your hands. Press down hard, and in one sweeping motion pull the steel lengthwise over the edge of the scraper. This burnishing action produces a fine edge—a slight burr—which is very effective for scraping.

3 Dovetails

Small table with dovetails
Cherry, designed and built by Eloise Rosas
Photo by Richard T. Conroy

TOOLS NEEDED

WORKBENCH
SQUARE
SCRIBE
DOVETAIL SAW
CHISEL
HAMMER
CABINET SCRAPER
PLANE

When King Tutankhamen's grave was opened, among other treasures a small chest was found, the sides of it fastened together with open dovetails. This piece was made about 3,350 years ago and there is every reason to believe that this was not the first dovetailed furniture built by a craftsman.

Once boards were split, carved, or cut from a trunk of wood, ways had to be found to accommodate the character of the new material. It was necessary to prevent the boards' natural tendency to warp. Boards expand and contract, and joints to allow such movement had to be invented. Since glues, especially all early ones, are useless on the end grain of wood, side grain had to be made to meet side grain. Faced with all this, the woodworker had very few options left. Way back in the past, somebody confronted with a board made a dovetail and found the ideal answer to a complex problem created by the new shape of wood. Nobody knows how long it took to make the first dovetail joint. Yours will require less than an hour.

When you select the two boards to be dovetailed, be aware they do not have to have the same thickness. It is very helpful, however, to choose quarter-sawed wood if possible. The vertical grain prevents warping, and without causing any problems the better looking side of each board can be used on the outside of the dovetail joint.

With plain-sawed wood there is no choice. The face must be on the outside, since this arrangement will tighten the joint as soon as the boards begin to warp—and warp they will. Remember, the face is the side of the board that once was facing toward the center of the trunk when it was still inside the tree.

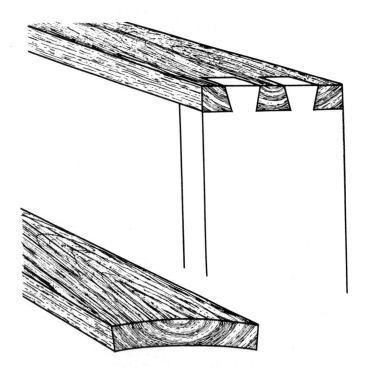

Mark the outsides clearly with an X and trace one board against the other. With an awl and square, score all around the future joint, in order to establish a base for the dovetails and pins. (The pins are the counterparts of the dovetails.) The score is the foothold for your chisel and saw.

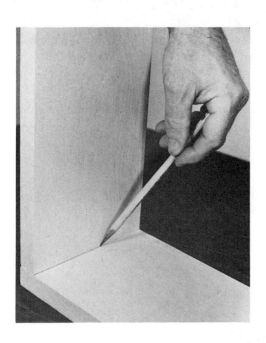

The number of dovetails to be made for the length of a joint is mostly an aesthetic matter. One more or one less will hardly make a difference in strength. However, it is an accepted practice to make the dovetails wider than the pins.

The angle of the dovetails is important. Too much slant will allow the dovetails to break, and too little slant will weaken the entire joint. The right amount is about 10 to 12 degrees.

With a pencil draw the dovetails between the end of the board and the score. Make certain to keep the spaces between the dovetails wider than the chisel you will use. After clamping the board vertically on to the workbench, use the square again to draw the top of every dovetail. Take a look and notice: Most of the lines you have just drawn appear to be in an angle to each other. From your position, standing in front of your workpiece, only a few look straight. The straight lines are the ones you are after.

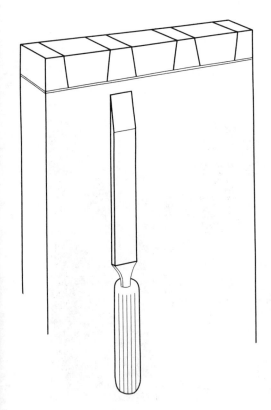

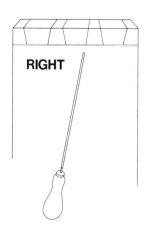
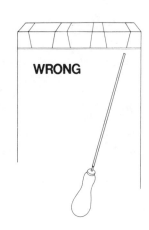

Your body should be placed behind the dovetail saw in order to see the future cut straight on. The less your body is in line with the saw and the cut you are making, the more difficult it will be to control the direction of the cut. For each cut you have to align your body again. Go ahead now and use your saw.

Two more cuts have to be made. Rearrange the board on your workbench. It should still be vertical, but this time place the board so that the grain is horizontal. Can you feel how the saw slips into the score? Cut the two corners off. Again, your body should be behind your saw.

Your chisel has two sides, each one serving a particular need. The flat side will preserve the wood you wish to keep; the chamfered side will push the unneeded wood away, usually crushing some of its fibers. In other words, the flat side always stays on the side of the wood to be preserved, except when making a mortise joint. We will come to this in another chapter.

When you remove the board from the clamp and place it flat on the workbench, you will discover that not only does the score serve well as a guide for the dovetail saw, it serves even better in guiding the chisel.

It would be wise at this point to take another look at the board. Make certain you are about to cut the spaces between the dovetails, not the dovetails. There is no need to drive the chisel through the whole board with the first hammerblow. A little bit at a time is much better; a sixteenth of an inch is about right. Be sure to hold the chisel vertically. Once you have removed the first layer of the wood between the dovetails, you need not use so much care in cutting away the remaining wood. The second time around, the chisel should be pointed inward to make certain that none of the remaining fibers will interfere with the close fit of the future joint.

 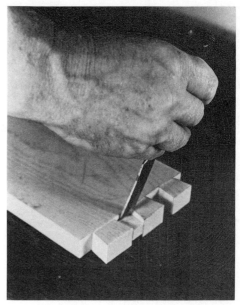

It does not matter if the recessed inner part of the joint will not touch its counterpart, since glue does not hold on end grain. It is important that side grain touch side grain, that the sides of the dovetails fit to the sides of the pins so that the glue can serve its purpose. If your dovetails look like the pictures, you have made the first half of a dovetail joint. *Congratulations!*

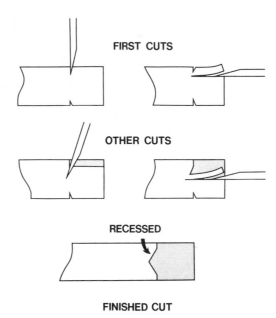

FIRST CUTS

OTHER CUTS

RECESSED

FINISHED CUT

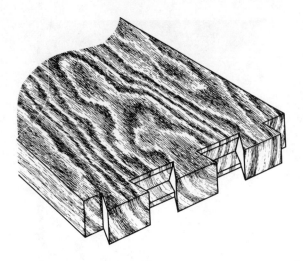

The next step requires the use of a well-sharpened pencil. Clamp the other board vertically onto your workbench with the outside mark facing you, and place the dovetailed board, with the outside marking facing up, on top. Trace the dovetails to establish the size of the future pins. Use your square again to draw the sides of the pins.

Do not cut yet. There is no way to trace with the pencil under the dovetail to mark the proper location for your cuts. The pencil, no matter how sharp, will only *outline* the dovetails. Do not cut on the lines unless you like a loose joint. The right way is to cut beside the lines, just outside them. The location of your body is still important.

Removing the wood from between the pins is done the usual way. The chisel is used vertically first and slanted inward for the rest of the cuts. Your aim is to produce similar recesses as those between the dovetails.

Are you ready? Fasten the board with the pins vertically onto the workbench. Place the board with the dovetails above it, and with very gentle tappings with the hammer join the two pieces together. Your first dovetail joint!

If you have done it right, the ends of the tails and the pins will be just a hair higher than the adjacent wood. This makes it very easy to clean the joint after gluing it. Use a plane and be careful not to round off the corners.

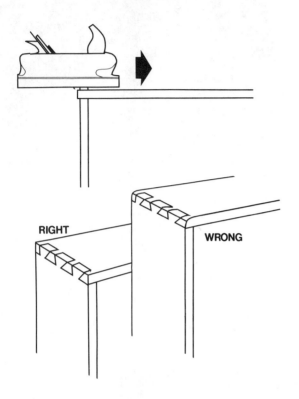

RIGHT

WRONG

The hidden dovetail joint came into being to fill a need created by a new trend in furniture making. Inspired by mosaics and stained-glass art, intarsia became one of the status symbols of the Renaissance.

Intarsia is a technique of decorating a surface with glued-on pieces of wood. Needless to say, the exposed end grain of open dovetails and pins did not provide a proper gluing base. Thus, hidden and—for some rare uses—double-hidden dovetail joints had to be invented and used.

You already know how to make the dovetails, but there is one difference: The tails of the hidden joint are one-third shorter. After you trace the part that will hold the pins on to the board that will have the tails, divide the length by three and score all around on the two-third mark.

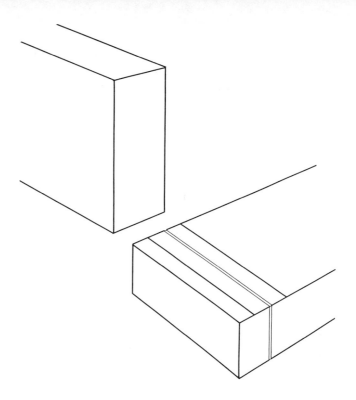

There is no need in any dovetail joint that the boards to be fastened together be of the same thickness. In fact, in a hidden joint the board with the pins is likely to be thicker than the board with the tails.

Draw the dovetails and cut as usual. Remove the wood between the dovetails and on the sides in the same way you did when making the open dovetail joint. When you are finished with the tails, fasten the counterpiece (the piece with the pins) vertically on to your workbench and place the dovetails on top. Naturally the face of the wood must be outside. Now trace the dovetails with a very sharp pencil.

You need one more score to mark the thickness of the board with the dovetails. This score is on the inside only. With the square draw the vertical lines of the future pins.

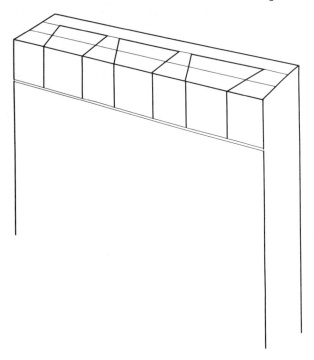

Just as with the open dovetail joint your saw should cut outside the tracing in order to assure a tight fit. Be sure you make only half the cut. *Be careful.* It is very easy to cut too deep.

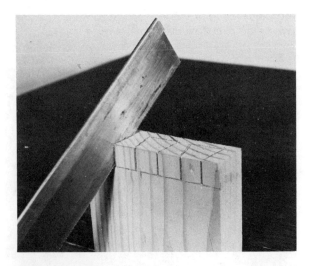

The rest of the cut is made with the cabinet scraper. Use a scraper the same thickness as the dovetail sawblade. Complete the task by hammering the scraper carefully down, using the existing half of the cut as a guide. Remember in the direction of its grain wood is very weak. Only a few fibers are in the way of the scraper, and these get pushed into the wood cells below.

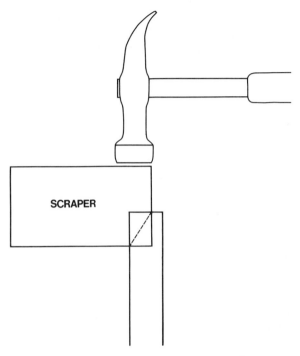

If the first and last cut on your joint is close to the edge of the board, it will be helpful to use a clamp for support. There is no need to tighten the clamp firmly, just make it hold.

Once you have made certain that all the cuts have been made all the way, place the wood face down on your workbench. The workbench should be clean and flat, and your chisel sharp. As usual, the score of the awl serves as a guide for the chisel. Do not forget that the flat side of the chisel faces toward the wood to be preserved.

The first cut is straight down. Carefully remove the first layer of wood. Only then should you aim the chisel a few degrees inward. The closer the chisel comes toward the bottom, the more carefully you should proceed. Keep the line showing the end of the dovetail. It should not be cut away.

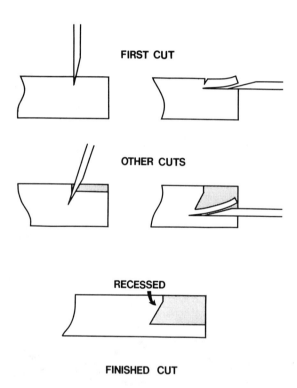

FIRST CUT

OTHER CUTS

RECESSED

FINISHED CUT

There is a good chance that the inner corners of the pins are not cut deep enough. Make certain they are clean and square before you join the two elements of the hidden dovetail together. If it looks like the picture, cheers to you. You just completed a hidden dovetail.

4 Wooden nails and dowels

Old chest with wooden nails
Partially painted spruce, Austrian
Photo by Richard T. Conroy

TOOLS NEEDED

WORKBENCH
HAMMER
DOVETAIL SAW
CHISEL
DRILL AND BIT
BRACE
DOWEL CENTERS
PLANE

A peg, a wooden nail driven into wood, may very likely be the oldest wood connection of all. One can easily imagine a cave dweller of some 25,000 years ago pushing a broken branch into a hole of a tree trunk. The hole is just there at the right time and the right spot. After hanging a wet fur on it for drying, the cave dweller steps back and, quite satisfied, admires the first coatrack.

Surely this was not the pegged joint we know now. There is a long way between the branch and a modern dowel, but the idea was and is the same. This first peg led to mortise-and-tenon joints, opened the way to bronze and iron nails and ultimately to rivets, steel bolts, and screws. Yet the wooden nail has never lost its usefulness. It is more compatible with wood than any other fastener. It does not corrode and, glued into place, it becomes one with its surroundings.

Before we make a modern dowel joint, inserting machine-made dowels into cylindrical holes, let's see how wooden nails were prepared and used in the past. Early drills produced conical holes. Conical holes in turn required a wedge-shaped wooden nail to fit.

This kind of nail was split from a block with a cleaver, chisel, or knife. The key to the success of the joint was the cross section of the nail used. If there was no danger of splitting the wood, any reasonably fitting nail with a square cross section was applied. The photo of such a nail, used in a very old chest, illustrates how it was done. This hardwood nail compressed the wood fibers around it on all four sides. The soft wood yielded and realigned itself to the shape of the nail, producing a tight fit. This glueless joint has held for many hundred years.

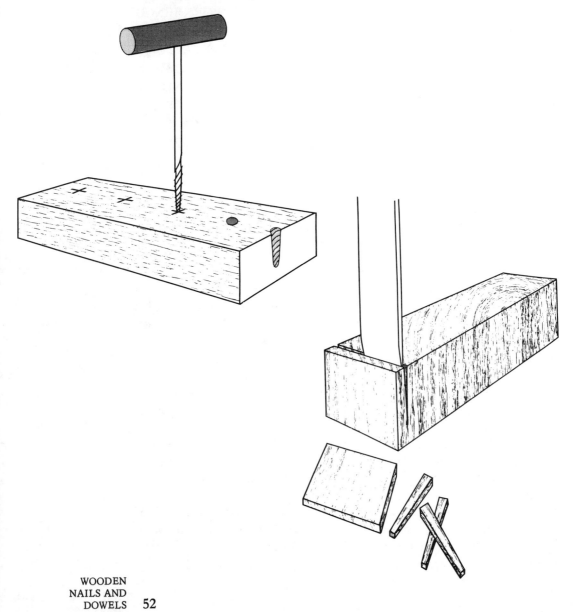

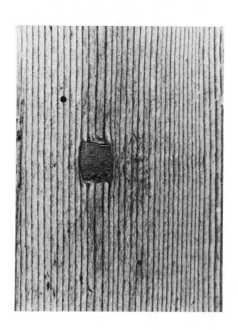

On the same chest a different nail was used to hold a narrow molding down. The cross section is rectangular; the fibers of the end grain are compressed while the side grain shows almost no sign of pressure; thus a split of the molding is avoided.

Once glues came into use, the wooden nail changed slightly. Quite often the squared peg was turned 45 degrees in order to allow the glue to penetrate into more side grain. This, however, raised the risk of splitting narrow pieces again. The problem was solved by chamfering the outer corners of the nail, creating in this process a sort of elongated hexagonal cross section. The flattened sides of the peg, in the round hole allowed the glue to stay where it was needed until the last moment, when the final tightening took place.

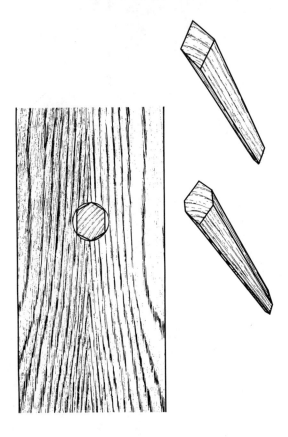

A dowel, round in cross section, in a cylindrical hole does not function like a wooden nail: At no time will it wedge itself into a tight fit. Therefore glue is needed. Instead of keeping the glue where it should be, however, the unprepared dowel does exactly the opposite. See for yourself. Put glue on a ¼-inch dowel and hammer it into a ¼-inch hole. Certainly you get the dowel in, but the glue does not go with it. Putting glue into the hole is even worse. The dowel will act as a piston pushing the glue down and, since liquids cannot be compressed more than a fraction, the glue on the bottom will prevent the dowel from going where it should. In order to make a good dowel joint, you have to reshape the modern dowel into something more like an old wooden nail.

Take the two boards you wish to join and arrange them as shown. Make certain the face of each board is on the right side, take a nail, and drive it almost all the way in so that the future joint will not slip. A large joint may need more than one nail. The place of each nail will later be taken by a dowel.

Draw a line indicating the center of the holes to be drilled and mark on it the distance you wish to hold between each dowel. As with the dovetail joint, aesthetic reasons will very likely determine the number of dowels you will use. Of course, in a highly stressed joint many dowels are needed.

The thickness of the dowel is usually one-third the thickness of the wood into which it is set. This allows for slight errors when you drill the holes. Use a bit the same size as the thickness of the dowel and drill all holes, saving the spot with the nail for later. The depth of the holes should be as shown in the picture or deeper.

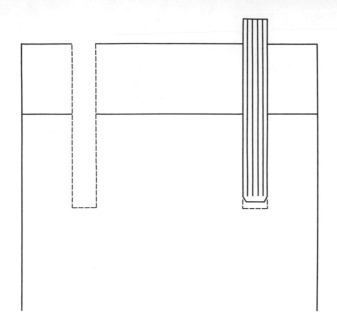

Pull out the nail, or nails, to separate the boards. Remove all wood chips and, using the nail again as a guide and fastener, assemble the joint as it was before cleaning.

Your dovetail saw will prove useful in preparing the dowels for gluing. The grooves made by the saw when you pull each dowel over it will allow the glue to rise between the dowel and the inside of the hole. If the dowel appears like a miniature fluted Greek column, it will be just fine.

One more preparation is needed before the dowel is ready to be used: Chamfer the edges with a chisel.

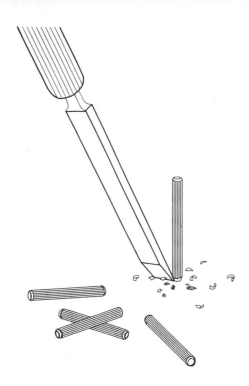

Make the dowel about ½ inch longer than the depth of the hole. The surplus can be cut off after gluing, and if the dowel mushrooms while you hammer it in, no harm will have been done.

This is the moment you have been waiting for. Put glue on the dowel—a few drops into the hole will also help—and drive the dowel in. Do not stop. The friction produces heat, heat cures the glue very fast, and if you hesitate, you find yourself with a well-glued dowel only halfway down.

If all dowels are in, there is no need to wait. Pull the nail or nails, drill, and insert a dowel wherever one is needed. Cut the surplus dowel heads off and clean with a plane.

Pictured is your open dowel joint.

To make a hidden dowel joint, one other tool is needed: dowel centers.

Whenever the end of a board cannot be used as a guide, as in this joint, it is very helpful if you mark and trace the setup with a sharp pencil.

Lay the upright piece aside and mark on the remaining board, within the outline, where the dowels will be. Do not drill yet.

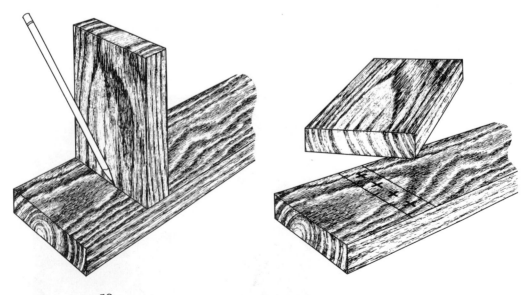

It is customary, on this side of the dowel joint, to drill only two-thirds down. There is a reason for this. Most woods do not thoroughly resist surplus glue that is pushed through their cells. Be very careful when you drive the dowels in. A hidden dowel joint does not look good with glue oozing out on the other side.

Estimating the depth of the holes to be drilled is not possible. A drill stop must be used. There are commercial drill stops available, but it is just as good if you make your own. Attach a piece of scrap wood to the drill, leaving only enough of the bit exposed beyond it that is exactly the depth of the desired hole. Drill all the way until the chuck touches the end grain. Cut and trim. Obviously the amount of the drill exposed will be the depth of the hole.

Now is the time to drill all holes and to insert the dowel centers.

 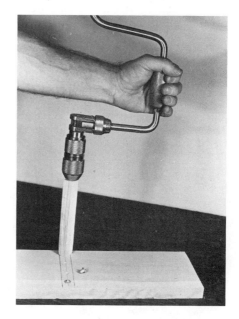

When you place the vertical board on to the dowel centers, use the outline for correct alignment. A tap with the hammer will press the bottom of the vertical piece onto the pins of the dowel centers, thus marking where to drill the next holes. Lay the upright piece aside and remove the dowel centers.

All dowels in a hidden dowel joint must have the same length. The chamfer on the lower end of the dowels should be made very small in order to preserve as much gluing surface as possible.

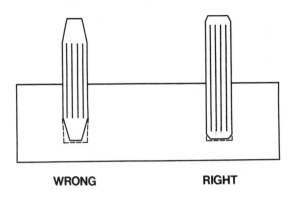

WRONG   **RIGHT**

Put glue into the holes and onto the low ends of the dowels. Tap the dowels in carefully, and make certain they all reach the bottom of the holes. Since you made all dowels the same length, you will immediately see if one dances out of line. Remove all surplus glue with a sponge or a wet cloth.

Now drill the holes into the other piece. If you're doing this for the first time, ask a friend to help. You cannot see from every side if you are drilling straight, and a pair of extra eyes is very helpful.* All holes must be deeper than the remaining length of the dowels and as straight as possible.

Once again, watch your markings. Put glue onto the dowels and into the holes, and join the two pieces. What a shame! All the work you have done, and nobody can see that this is a hidden dowel joint.

The helpful eyes in the picture belong to photographer Simin Hassanzadeh.

WOODEN
NAILS AND
DOWELS

5 Mortises and tenons

Dining table with mortises and tenons
Walnut and cherry, designed and built by the author
Photo by Richard T. Conroy

TOOLS NEEDED

WORKBENCH
SQUARE
SCRIBE
DOVETAIL SAW
CHISEL
HAMMER
CROSSCUT SAW
PLANE

Exodus 26:15 gives instructions for a cabinetmaker:

And thou shalt make boards for the tabernacle of shittim wood standing up.

Ten cubits shall be the length of one board, and a cubit and a half shall be the breadth of one board.

Two tenons shall there be in one board, set in order one against another: Thus shalt thou make for all the boards of the tabernacle.

That long ago tenons were already in use. There is a good reason for this: No other joint is as versatile and many-sided. It comes in hidden and open versions. The tenon can be fixed or movable, only fastened with a wedge to the piece that holds the mortise. It can be almost any size: It can be used on a jewelry chest or on a barn. If it's properly made, it will always serve well.

MORTISES
AND
TENONS

It may take an hour the first time to produce a simple mortise-and-tenon joint. After that, any time spent will depend on the complexity of the undertaking.

The first step in making this wood connection is to mark clearly where and in which direction the pieces have to fit together.

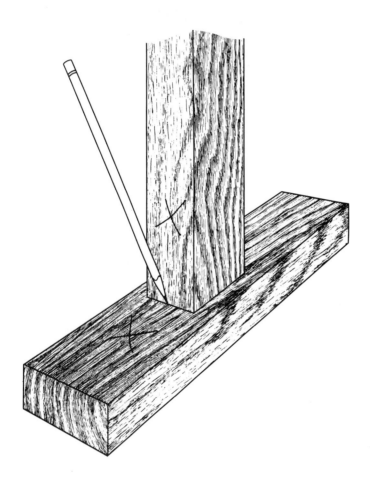

Make the X mark on the piece that will have the tenon high enough to be certain not to remove it in cutting the first layers of the wood. Trace the height of the horizontal member against the upright piece.

With square and awl score all around. The score will help you cut on the right place with the dovetail saw.

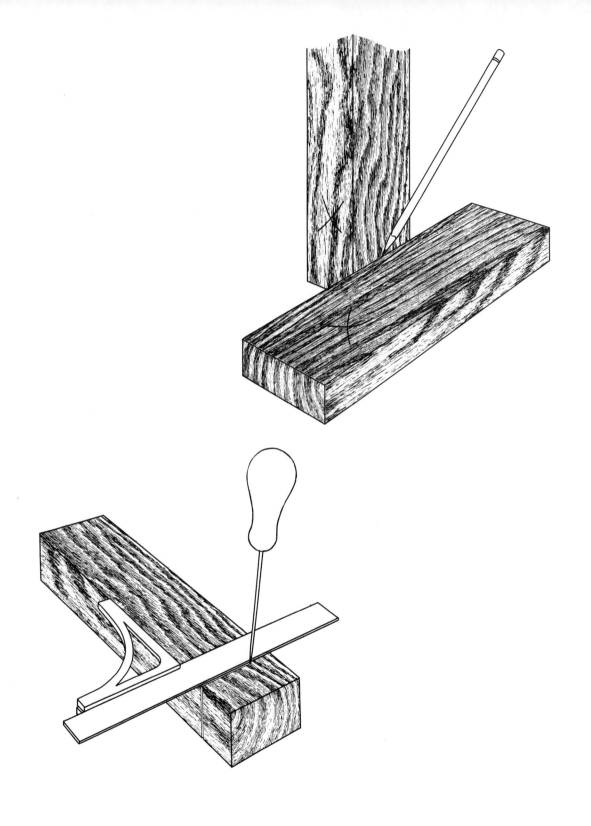

Fasten the scored piece vertically to the workbench, with the end becoming the tenon pointing up. With a pencil draw two lines to divide the top—which, when turned around, will be the bottom of the tenon—into three equal parts. The dotted lines show how your marks should look.

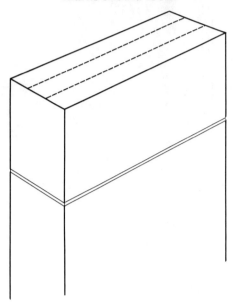

Do not stop drawing. There is more to be done. Divide the outer thirds in two and extend these lines around the corners down to the score. The unbroken lines show how these new lines should look. Cut on the solid line.

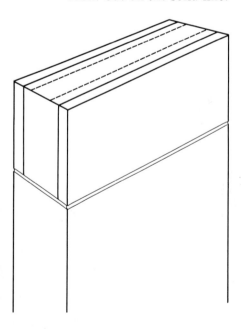

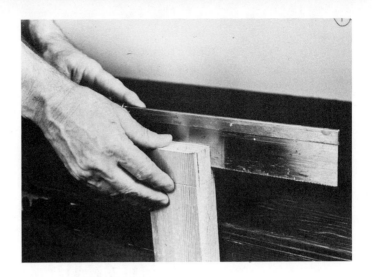

The tenon, the male part of this joint that will be fitted into the mortise, is usually two-thirds the thickness of the wood from which it is made. The width of the tenon is another matter, depending on the kind of wood one uses and where it is used. Remember, wood *does* shrink.

The table in the picture below has several mortise-and-tenon joints, each allowing the wood to move, but the tenon of the side-board connected with the top of the table is only divided into four small units in order to preserve the structural strength of the table-top. Shrinkage and expansion is taken care of with the alignment of all the grain in the same direction.

Other furniture is also made this way.

Only when the woodgrains of a joint are crossed does shrinkage and expansion become critical.

Tenons of softwoods should not be wider than about 4 inches. With most hardwoods which shrink less, the limit is about 7 inches. Decide for yourself how wide your tenon should be, according to the design you are working on, and cut.

Remove the tenon from its vertical position and place it flat on the workbench. Using the score as a guide for the dovetail saw cut all around. Keep the small pieces; you will need them later.

Align the two pieces with each other again, and with a sharp pencil trace the tenon on to its counterpart.

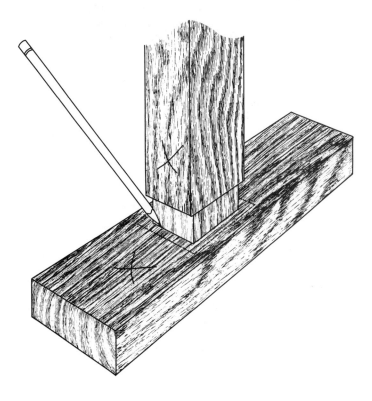

Remember what you have just drawn is only an outline. Your chisel must be used inside of your lines to assure a tight fit of the tenon. As usual, the flat side of the chisel stays with the side of the wood to be preserved. Chisel straight down and carefully remove the first layer of wood.

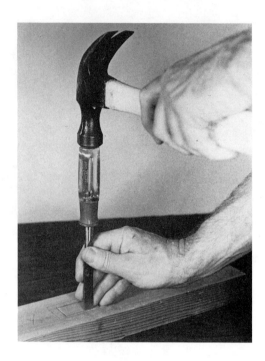

It will be well worth your time to take a good look at the following picture. The chisel is used straight down as always, but whenever there is a need to scoop wood out, the flat side of the tool should meet the wood to be removed. With the flat side down the chisel will dig itself in, making it very hard to control the cutting.

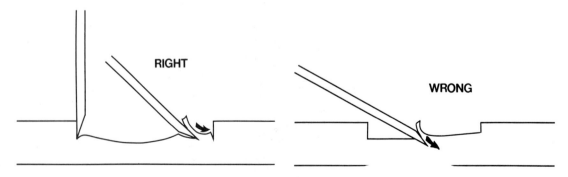

RIGHT

WRONG

Once the first layer of wood has been removed, the vertical cuts into the future mortise are only made where the end grain is. In softwood especially, the side grain is so weak it is not worth cutting. Just scoop the hole out and let the side grain break wherever it does. There is no need for concern about the rough sides of the mortise. The tenon, when driven in, will clean it and will also align itself in the process.

Should you decide to cut the mortise all the way from one side, make sure you put a piece of scrap wood underneath to protect the workbench. It is also a good idea to fasten the workpiece firmly down; otherwise the chisel will break some of the woodfibers on the bottom of the opening. Most of the time it is better to cut the mortise from both sides. The square with its adjustable blade is a good measuring device for transferring the outline of the mortise from one side to the other.

After the mortise is cut, insert the tenon. Be certain that all markings line up the right way. It may be wise to use a hand screw to prevent the piece with the mortise from splitting. The tenon should be tight. Hammer it in carefully, just a bit, not all the way.

Stop and turn the whole thing around. While the tenon moves down into the mortise, see how it rolls away all fibers not needed for a tight fit. Turn the piece back and use your hammer again.

The last part has to be watched carefully. Just before the tenon emerges, clean the inside of the mortise. If you do not, the tenon will do it for you. The result, however, will not be very neat.

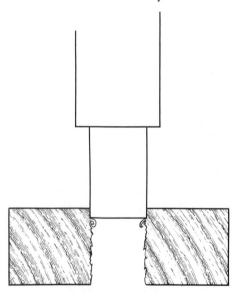

Remove the hand screw and take a look at the collar. (The collar is the section in which the original width of the wood ends and the tenon begins.) Most likely the parts will not fit. One side of the collar may be too high, or it may not be as square as it should be.

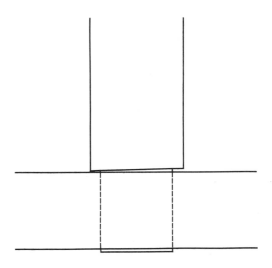

The activity of fitting the collar to its counterpart is called "cutting it together." Usually we cut things apart. There is always an exception and this is the one for sawing.

Fasten the joint flat to the bench and saw between collar and mortise. Be careful—*do not cut into the tenon.* Continue to do this on all four sides. Sawing this way, using the wood with the mortise as a guide, you create an even space between collar and counterpart. The thickness of this space is that of the sawblade. Remove the sawdust and drive the tenon in. Does it fit? If not, repeat the procedure until it does. It helps if you use a square to measure the angle between tenon and mortise.

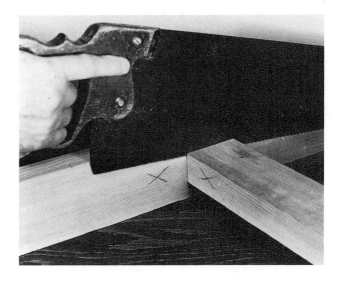

A mortise-and-tenon joint is designed to carry high loads. It is the strongest of all joints. Not only does side grain meet side grain for a good gluing arrangement but, where glue cannot hold, wedges are inserted for additional strength. Even the collar serves to stiffen the joint.

Take the joint apart. If necessary, remove the scratches made by the saw on the piece with the mortise. This is easily done with a plane.

The purpose of the wedges is to widen the tenon. Make sure you have the wedges close enough to the edge to allow the outside of the tenon to flex.

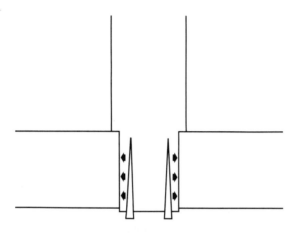

Fasten the tenon vertically and cut the openings for the wedges. Remember the small pieces left after you cut the tenon? Take one now and make the wedges from it. The grain in the wedge must be vertical. Make the slot for the wedge wide enough!

Glue the tenon into the mortise. Glue the wedges into the tenon, tightening both with a hammer. Clean the bottom of the joint; the saw and plane are the right tools for this. Lean back and admire your mortise-and-tenon joint.

One more word about wedges. In mortise-and-tenon joints they are used in a wide variety of ways. You may invent one for yourself someday. There are wedges, or pins, glued sideways through the whole joint, to prevent the tenon from slipping out of the mortise, In a tusk tenon the wedge is not glued at all. Friction is holding it in place, and occasionally it must be retightened.

MORTISES
AND
TENONS

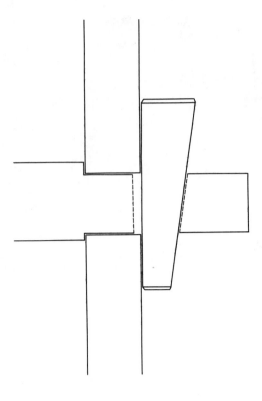

The most difficult mortise-and-tenon joint is the hidden one. To get the wedges just right takes practice. They touch the deepest part of the mortise first, and in one fluid motion the tenon is driven into its own wedges. If the wedges are too big, the joint will not go together. Needless to say, you will not get it apart either. You may as well cut it off and make a new one. Also the tenon has to be shorter than the depth of the mortise to allow space for surplus glue. Good luck.

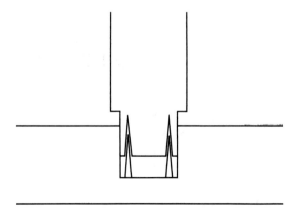

Frames and panels 6

Cabinet with drawer and doors, paneled
Partially painted fir, American
Photo by Richard T. Conroy

TOOLS NEEDED

WORKBENCH   SCRIBE
CROSSCUT SAW   DOVETAIL SAW
RIPSAW   CHISEL
SCRUB PLANE   HAMMER
JOINTER PLANE   GROOVING PLANE
SMOOTHING PLANE   CLAMPS OR HAND SCREWS
SQUARE

For thousands of years heavy or large furniture did not exist. Dining facilities or night beds were a part of the architecture built into the house, if there was a house. A Roman dining table (called a *Mensa*) for instance, was made of stone and not mobile at all. The stone slabs still used on the altars of some Christian churches remind us of this.

The German word Möbel, derived from the Latin *mobilis,* aptly describes such early furniture as small chests, day recliners, and folding chairs. The early Renaissance, however, brought a dramatic change in furniture design. Dining tables became wooden structures immobile enough to rival most Roman *mensae*. Beds became wooden houses within the house, often equipped with stairs leading up to them, and rooves covering them.

The new size of furniture required wider boards, made of several pieces glued together. Harnessing the aggravated warping, shrinking, and expanding of this material spawned a whole new technology. Frames and other supports came into being.

An unframed panel, such as that used for a tabletop, will serve well as an illustration of how this new technology worked. The panel will expand and reduce itself whenever the weather changes. It will also warp. The amount of this movement is determined by the width of the panel and the type of wood used.

For a medium-sized table the easiest way to stabilize the top is to glue the middle down, supporting the glue joint with dowels if necessary. The sides of the panel are left to move back and forth, riding the frame or skirt. This system works especially well if plain-sawed boards are used. They must be face up. The natural tendency to warp down will keep this tabletop where it should be.

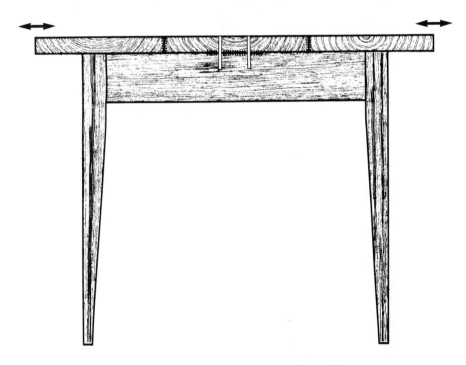

All larger panels need more support, and quite often sliding blocks are the best way to provide it. Such blocks can easily be cut from a piece of scrap wood. One or more sliding blocks glued to the underside of the panel are needed. Recesses, carved with a chisel into the skirt of the table, provide the counterpart for the fingers of the blocks to slide in, out, or sideways.

FRAMES
AND
PANELS

The frame prevents the tabletop from warping down. The blocks keep it from warping up, and the fingers also allow the movement necessary to prevent cracking the panel.

Either the middle or the side of the tabletop must be glued to the table frame.

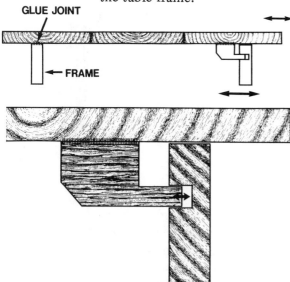

Another way to stabilize large panels is to use dovetailed runners. After the panel has been slid on to the dovetails, it should be secured with wooden pegs. A few drops of glue on one end of the runners will serve the same purpose.

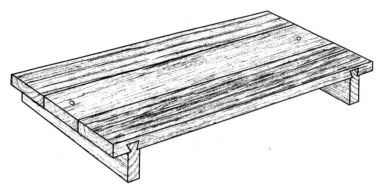

The most useful and common way to stabilize panels is by framing. Since the size of a frame is only limited by the length of wood and not by the width, the possibilities for making large furniture are almost limitless.

Boards used for furniture making are usually rough-cut. Take a close look at them and see how each piece has taken on its very own shape. While they were drying out, a few twists developed; the more dense fibers left the wood thicker in some areas than in other places where there are soft fibers. More often than not, the wood is not straight at all. Do not worry, wood like this is normal.

Be generous when selecting wood for a panel. Choose boards that are longer, wider, and thicker than you will ultimately need.

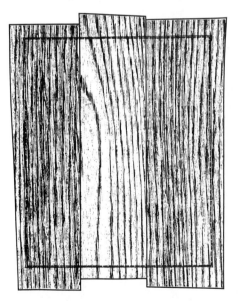

Lay the pieces side to side—if they are plain sawed, lay them face up—and make certain to look at the grain. Like the scales of a fish, grain is arranged in layers heading in one direction. All boards in

FRAMES
AND
PANELS

your future panel must be lined up accordingly. In case of doubt, use a plane. Planing in the right direction will produce a clean surface. The other way, the blade of the plane will undercut and pull the wood fibers up; this is not what you need.

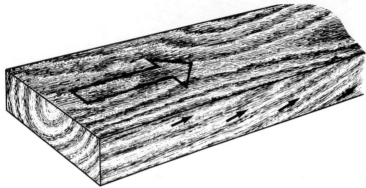

Mark your boards. If there are many it is wise to use numbers. Take two boards at a time to prepare the edges for gluing. Clamp the boards tightly together, edge up, to the workbench. The edge should be about 1 inch higher than the top of the bench.

Once again, the placement of your body becomes important. If you are right-handed, have the boards to your right and ahead of you. Your right hand will guide the plane, and your left hand will hold the plane in front. Keep your shoulders above the plane and your face looking down, lined up with it. For a left-hander things are reversed, as in the picture.

It is obvious that the large jointer plane will make planing long joints easy, but shorter joints can be done quite well with a smaller plane.

Now push, walking the plane from one end to the other. It is a good practice to begin each stroke holding down the front of the plane while the rear of the tool is not yet in contact with the workpiece. The end of the stroke requires just the opposite: The rear of the plane should be held down. If you plane this way, you can avoid rounding off the ends of the joint or leaving a crest in the middle of it.

A glance along the edge of the joint is very helpful in seeing how well you have done. There is no need to be concerned if the joint is slightly cocked to the left or right. If you rotate the boards to match the markings you have made before, they will complement each other.

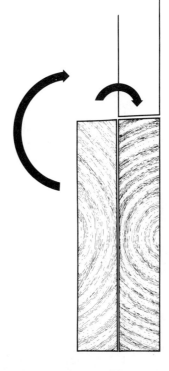

The gluing is easy work. Clamp the boards lightly together after putting glue on both edges. Tighten the clamps a bit more and see how the surplus glue settles outside the joint. The droplets of the glue will look like a chain of pearls.

Many glue joints need hours to harden, and some have to be left overnight to reach ultimate strength. In case of doubt, wait.

Fasten your panel on to the workbench. Clamps, strips of thin wood nailed around the panel, and other devices will do. Bench-dogs are best. Since the panel is not yet flat, you may have to support it with a few small shims.

The first order of business is to flatten the back side of the panel. At this point the thickness of the wood may seem excessive. This is true, but remember, you could not purchase thin rough-cut boards. Besides this, there are many bumps and warps in the wood that need to be planed away.

The scrub plane, with its very convex cutting edge, will do this in a hurry, especially if you occasionally cut in a 45-degree angle across the grain.

If the panel is large, the jointer plane serves well to flatten it. The less convex cutting edge of this plane will remove most of the ridges left by the rather coarse treatment the scrub plane has given the wood. A small panel is usually worked with a general smoothing plane for this purpose. Even with the large panel, the final cleaning and flattening is done with a fine smoothing plane. When you have finished with the back side, turn the panel around and plane the front side.

Needless to say, even the best smoothing plane has a convex cutting blade and will leave the panel slightly wavy. You may not see the waves going parallel with the grain, but you can feel them with your fingertips. Be proud of this, this kind of surface is the telltale mark of handmade furniture. Choose only straight-grained wood for the frame. If you choose lesser wood, the pain you inflict on yourself when you cut grooves into it is not worth the saving you may have obtained.

Since you have the panel, you are able to determine the size of the frame for it. After planing the material to the right dimension, cut each section slightly longer than needed with the crosscut saw. If you have good wood, the grooves are easy to cut.

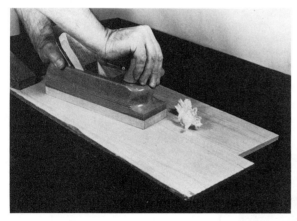

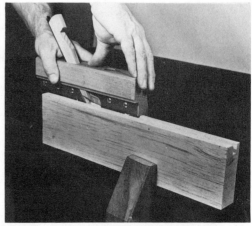

The corners of the frame can be joined in many ways. The frame could be mitered and pegs or splines used to hold the corners together. One of the several versions of lap joints would also be suitable. A mortise-and-tenon joint seems to be the best choice, as it is strong, and easy to cut and assemble to create a nice clean look.

The width of each end of the frame is traced onto its counterpart. This will establish the depth of the mortises and the length of the tenons. The thickness of the tenons should be about the same as the edge of the panel to be inserted into the groove of the frame.

In order to get a tight fit, cut the tenons a hair thicker than the size of the groove. If the tenons turn out too tight, a few taps with the hammer will compress the wood fibers to make it just right. Be aware that the tenons are narrower than the frame; the wood removed from the groove is missing.

The mortises are as wide as the groove of the frame, and the inside of the groove is useful as a guide for the saw. Cut twice for each mortise, but not too deep. Remember, the tenon is narrower than the frame. Remove the surplus wood with a chisel.

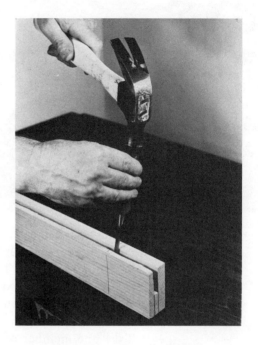

Assemble the frame and square it. The inside edges of the frame, opposite to each other, must be parallel. You may have to push the frame slightly apart on one side in order to make it right.

Fasten the frame to the bench with a clamp, securing each mortise-and-tenon joint in order to avoid slippage. Then cut each joint together. All eight cuts, please. Mark or number each corner.

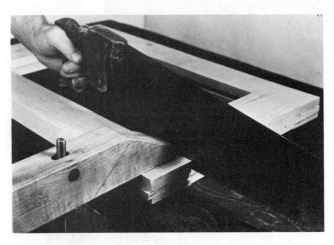

After you clean out the sawdust, tighten the frame and measure how much space is left for the panel. If the panel is too tight, the whole effort of building the frame will be wasted. The panel must have room to expand into. Since you know the hardness and density of the wood you have been working with you can decide how much to cut.

Take one member of the frame out, insert the panel, and re-assemble the frame, making certain that all joints close. The panel will not be glued—it cannot escape. Glue the frame only. Clean and trim. Here is the first part of a paneled piece of furniture.

Woodcarving

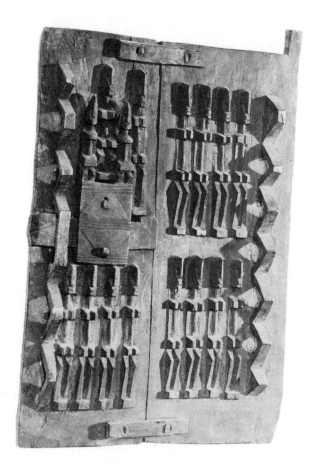

Granary door
Dogon, Africa
Courtesy of Morton Ehudin
Photo by Richard T. Conroy

TOOLS NEEDED

WORKBENCH
SHALLOW GOUGE
DEEP GOUGE
FLAT CHISEL
MALLET

A few years ago I had the pleasure of observing a woodcarver from West Africa who demonstrated his craft at the Museum of African Art in Washington, D.C. He was a master. It did not matter what he carved but how, and with what, which made him a kin to all woodcarvers. His tools, made by his village blacksmith, could have been taken out of the hands of the ancient Greek sculptor Praxiteles. They could have been borrowed from Tilman Riemenschneider of medieval Europe. The Japanese temple carver Jōhō of the Fujiware period would have been just as comfortable with them, as would the many unknown Tlingit carvers of the American Northwest. Woodcarving tools and techniques have been, and are, the same everywhere. Unless wood changes, there will be no surprises in the future.

There are only a few kinds of carving chisels. A deep gouge, sometimes called veiner, is used to remove the bulk of the wood. A shallow gouge helps to cut the ridges left by the first chisel. The third tool, a flat chisel with two beveled sides, serves to clean flat and convex surfaces. For concave surfaces one of the gouges will do. Some woodcarvers also use a V groove, or parting chisel, for deep and narrow cuts. However, more often than not, the aforementioned tools serve this purpose quite well. These chisels come in all sizes.

Mallets made of wood, heavy for wide chisels and light for narrow ones, preserve the wooden handles of the chisels for a while, but sooner or later both have to be replaced. Mallets and handles are meant to wear out.

Yes, there are people who take a block of wood and cut right into it, having only a vague idea how the final outcome may look. Some actually succeed and hold a masterpiece in their hands after they have stopped carving. I would advise you to make a drawing first. A drawing, no matter how imperfect, clarifies and separates the options available in a given piece of material. Carving means to cut away what you do not need, leaving what you would like to have. If what you like to have is not still inside the block or panel of wood, you cannot get it. Make certain you have a chance to succeed. Make a drawing.

The difference between carving an all-around piece or a panel is visual only. A panel is worked on a flat plane from the outside in. A round piece with its curved surface appears to be different, but like the panel it is also carved from the outside in.

In technical terms what you carve is secondary; what is important is that you do it in the right sequence. Slaithong Schmutzhart, a sculptor and furniture maker, will carve a panel to demonstrate how it is done. The panel, one of two, will later be used to fill the doors of a small framed cabinet. Is your drawing ready? Transfer your pricture onto the wood. Use a deep gouge or a parting chisel to draw the picture again, this time not with lines but with deep cuts.

You will find that one side of your chisel, whether it is a parting tool or a deep gouge, makes a very clean cut, while the other side produces a totally opposite result. Knowing wood, this is no surprise. It is easy to cut with the grain, but hard to go against it. There are two solutions available for you. One is to use the gouges to cut from the top down into the wood. This way you cannot get under the grain, and thus the problem is avoided.

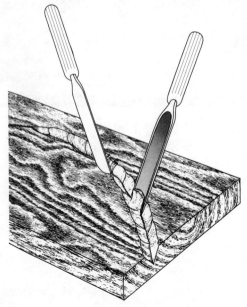

The parting tool is the other solution. If you want to use it, you will have to carve in two directions. The first journey, down the line, will leave one clean and one ragged edge. On the return trip, going back to where you came from, cut only the ragged edge, this time carving into the grain and not against it. Your reward will be two clean edges.

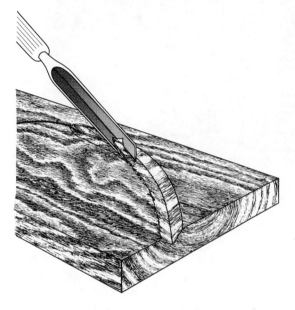

Do not carve on the wrong spot. Take a very good look before taking the next step.

The background of your design has to be separated from the foreground. This is done best by removing—recessing, that is—the wood between the positive parts of the picture. In the panel shown, the negative space is pushed back, and the leaves, flowers, and stems are left standing.

At this point, your carving will look like a miniature mesa landscape. To separate the flowers, or whatever you have carved, from one another is easy. Just tilt some of the upper planes and a clear picture will emerge.

The light illuminating your work should come from the side that will ultimately be the top of your finished piece. This arrangement will help you compose your carving while you work on it. If an item—say, a leaf—is too small, tilt it toward the light. The light shining on it will make it appear larger. Slanting an item away from the light will create a shadow, making this part of your composition look smaller.

Depending on the thickness of the wood, the process of recessing, tilting, and shaping may be repeated many times before a pleasant result is reached. At all times great care should be taken to avoid undercutting the grain. A woodcarving is like a roof with shingles: It functions very well if the chisel, like the water, moves from top down. Coming from the bottom up, chisel and water do more harm than good.

Keep the edges of the chisels clear if you can help it. You should never allow a tool to get buried in the material.

The design of the furniture in which the woodcarving is used will help you to decide when to stop. Totally clean is not always beautiful.

This panel will be painted in bright, cheerful colors. The chiselmarks are left deliberately to enhance the brilliance of the color.

8   Curved wood

Support from the bow of a former Chesapeake oyster boat
Maple
Photo by the author

TOOLS NEEDED

WORKBENCH
CROSSCUT SAW
RIPSAW
TURNING SAW
SPOKESHAVE
CABINET SCRAPER

A fifty-century B.C. Greek *Klismos* chair with its graceful curves and a good modern American rocking chair have the same ingredients. For each chair the maker needed an artist's eye in terms of design, and an engineer's touch for structural integrity. To build such wooden structures was, and is, a formidable challenge.

In the beginning, curved wood was the material of shipwrights. They were the leaders and inventors in this field. It was recognized very early that an ugly ship does not sail well, and a ship structurally unsound may sink. The shipwright's knowledge of the interaction of beauty and function turned out to be invaluable for all woodworkers. Never was a curved rib of a ship made of straight-grained wood, and the rocker of a rocking chair should not be built out of it. Long grain is strength, and short grain is weakness.

No original *klismos* chair exists today, but we know from pictures painted on ceramic vases how it looked. It is obvious that

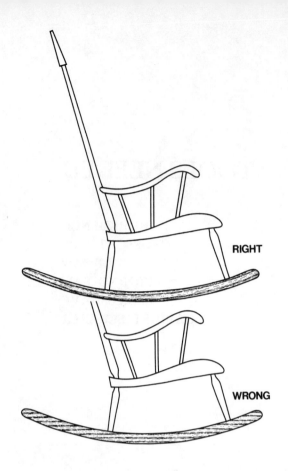

RIGHT

WRONG

straight-grained wood was not used to build it. Lamination and steam bending, processes of modern mass production, were unknown at this time. There is only one answer: curved wood. Fortunately, even today, many hardwoods, especially fruitwoods, more often grow curved than straight, providing us with an abundance of material for curved parts.

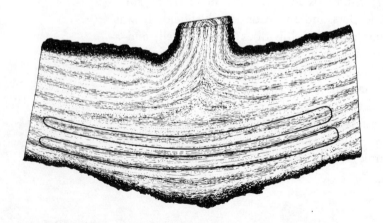

If it is possible to carry a load through unbroken long grain in a curved piece, or a curved part of a piece of furniture that is not under stress, straight-grained wood is sufficient. It will serve well without breaking. Any advantage gained in not having to look for just the right piece of wood, however, will be lost, since finishing a curved part made of straight-grained wood is more complex and time-consuming.

Making a Queen Anne leg will demonstrate this point. A leg such as this curves in more than one plane, and it is necessary to make a pattern to serve as an accurate guide. Bruce Gibson, who illustrated this book, has in his hand such a template made of cardboard.

 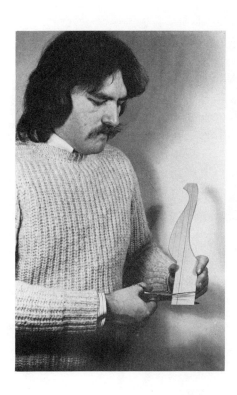

The wood used for making the leg should be cut longer and wider than the final size of the leg. The extra length is needed for clamping the piece to the workbench, and the additional width will allow the saw to cut without interruption. This will make the cleaning and finishing much easier.

Trace two adjacent sides of the future leg onto the wood, fasten the piece vertically, and cut on the outside of the line. The remaining line will serve later as a guide for the spokeshave. You must stand behind your saw, keeping the saw blade perpendicular to the wood at all times. Make all curved cuts first. You will need to use your template several times, depending on which piece you cut off first. For the straight cuts a common handsaw with its wide blade works better than the turning saw used for the curves.

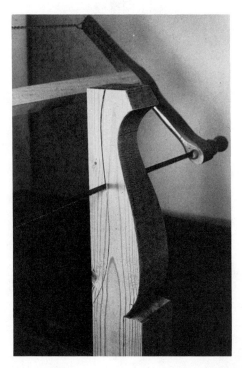

Take the workpiece from its vertical position and fasten it horizontally to the workbench. Now is the time to think and work like a woodcarver. Remember, cutting into the grain from the bottom up does not work. Like a woodcarving chisel, the spokeshave is always used to cut from top down. You will find that making ends meet with the opposite cut on the bottom is difficult. Before you cut too much, use a cabinet scraper. After all, this tool only scrapes; it cannot undercut. Using the scraper is a slow but safe way to work. No matter which tool you use, the direction of your effort smoothing this leg will change many times. The arrows show you the way.

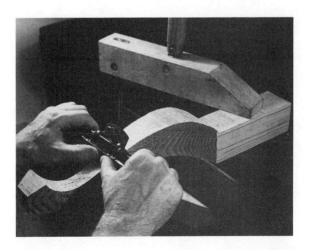

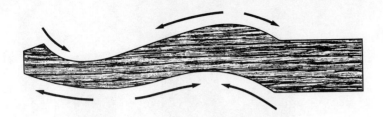

The final cleaning is up to you, depending on your particular preference. Should it be destined for part of a table whose straight parts are finished with a plane, consider a piece of glass as a tool. On cleanly broken glass at least one edge is razor sharp and serves better than the best cabinet scraper.

Well—three more legs to go.

Design 9

A hanging cabinet for a photographer
Mahogany, designed and built by Frederick L. Wall
Photo by Simin Hassanzadeh

TOOLS NEEDED

PAPER
PENCILS
COMMON SENSE

If you have the nagging suspicion that you missed learning about another fifty joints or so, be assured that what you now know enables you to build any properly designed piece of furniture you can think of. One exception to this is veneer work, which is a world in itself and is not covered in this book.

The many other joints you may have seen or heard of are only derivatives of the basic connections. Take a finger joint, for example. It is a poor cousin of dovetails, invented to accommodate a machine.

Have you ever seen New England furniture of the last century made with beautiful triangular pins set against wide tails? They look different and are harder to make, but although this Chinese joint was imported from Asia by American sailors, it is still simply a dovetail joint.

Another source for unusual connections is the combination of two or more basic joints. A butterfly joint, for instance, is two dovetails and a lap joint. The first is well known to us, and the lap joint is nothing but two pieces of wood glued crosswise or lengthwise together, with side grain touching side grain.

Now back to the legs. Their length will determine if a table or bench is in your immediate future. The construction of each is about the same. Make certain the upper part of the legs is large enough to accommodate tenons, otherwise use dowels.

If a drawer is involved, usually in a table, the skirt should be cut and the cutout used as a frontpiece for the drawer. Needless to say, a support has to be added to tie the skirt together, which also serves as a runner for the drawer. These pieces are simply glued into position. There is no need for any dowels or complicated joining.

DINING TABLE

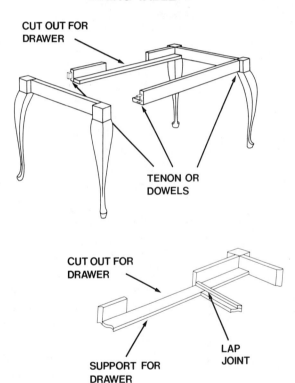

CUT OUT FOR DRAWER

TENON OR DOWELS

CUT OUT FOR DRAWER

SUPPORT FOR DRAWER

LAP JOINT

The drawer is dovetailed together with the lower part of the frontpiece serving as a stop to prevent the drawer from being pushed in too far. In order to allow for shrinkage or expansion, the bottom of the drawer is never glued into the grooves.

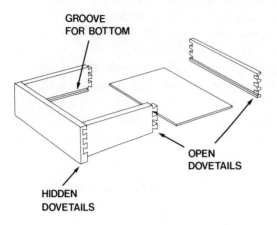

GROOVE
FOR BOTTOM

OPEN
DOVETAILS

HIDDEN
DOVETAILS

DRAWER

For making and installing the top of the table or bench, consult the beginning of Chapter 6.

The chair in the picture is, like a table, bench, or drawer, very standard. This is how most of these pieces of furniture are constructed. Certainly if you work hard enough to find it, there is a more complicated way to do business, however, there is no need to do so.

This does not mean you should not use your imagination. You could, for instance, curve the front piece of the chair forward to compensate visually for the two rearward-curved pieces supporting the back. If you decide to eliminate the lower structure of the chair, you may have to use tenons instead of dowels to hold the legs in place. All this or the addition of armrests does not alter the concept around which this chair is designed.

The seat allows even more options for your inventiveness. An unframed panel could be glued on to the skirt, the same way as the top on to a small table. The same panel could be trimmed to fit into the chair, leaving the upper edges of the skirt and the tops of the front legs exposed. A few blocks, glued to the inside of the skirt, would keep the seat from slipping down. A frame that has been upholstered could be inserted this way also. How about caning?

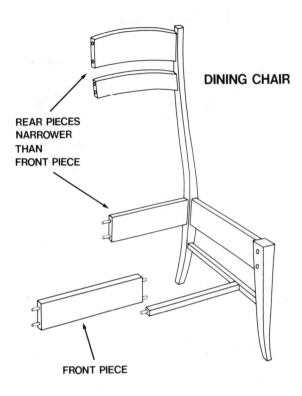

DINING CHAIR

REAR PIECES
NARROWER
THAN
FRONT PIECE

FRONT PIECE

The chest shows another basic way of constructing furniture, this time a container. The leg frame is made of several boards, glued together, mitered, and supported by corner blocks. The floor or bottom of the chest is an unframed panel fitted into its support but not glued to it. The body of this piece is dovetailed on all four corners to allow the wood to rise when expanding and to settle down when shrinking.

If the body of the chest needs to be glued to the leg frame, which is not always the case, the glue is applied between the inside of the leg frame and the lower outside of the body. The floor is left free to expand and contract, as is the top of the chest if you choose a frame for it. Many chests have no frame on top. Instead, the lid is made of choice quarter-sawed boards to avoid warping.

How about painting and carving this piece?

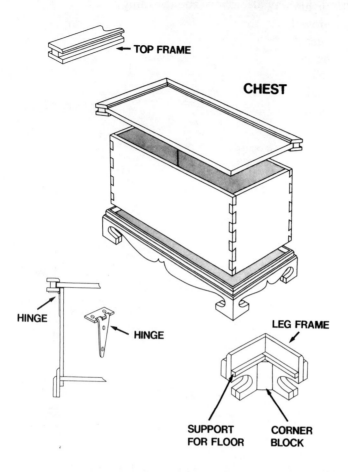

TOP FRAME

CHEST

HINGE

HINGE

LEG FRAME

SUPPORT
FOR FLOOR

CORNER
BLOCK

All large pieces of furniture, such as wardrobes, were and are built in sections stacked onto each other. There are two ways to do this. A highboy is basically two complete pieces, one sitting on top of the other. The other way is shown in the picture of the paneled cabinet. This cabinet, although it, too, is small enough to be built in one piece, has been left in several sections so it can be taken apart and transported with great ease when necessary. All dowels in this cabinet are glued on one end only.

The leg frame is one piece, constructed similarly to that of the chest. The floor panel is only partly glued, or attached with dowels, in order to allow for movement.

The left door and side panel, hinged to each other, are one section; as are the right door and side panel. The back, a frame with two panels in it and a few dowels on each side, is another part. The dowels are prepared to fit holes drilled into the side panels.

The last section, the counter, slides easily into the dowels fastened on top of the side panels. This arrangement holds the whole cabinet together. Gravity, and the fact that each section braces the other, makes a remarkably rigid structure.

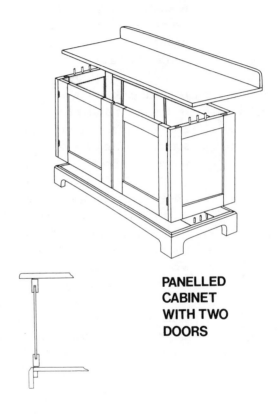

PANELLED CABINET WITH TWO DOORS

Once you have determined what kind of furniture you are going to build, you must also decide early if your piece will be stained, lacquered, shellacked, oiled, waxed, or painted. The nature and construction of wooden furniture demands careful thought here. A panel, for example, has its edges buried in the grooves of the frame. You must stain and polish the whole panel before it is inserted. Should you fail to do so, the panel will show bare wood whenever it contracts.

This is not the only problem. It is also impossible to do a neat staining job in a corner. The frame itself should be finished on the inside edge, the one with the groove, before final assembly. After the frame is glued, planed, and trimmed, the outside of it is finished. In other words, work from the inside out.

There is an even better reason for finishing the surfaces of furniture before final assembly: surplus glue. Quite often surplus glue, even if immediately wiped off, fills the pores of unstained wood and spoils the effectiveness of stain and other finishes. The result is a very spotty finish. If the wood is finished already, however, the glue can be wiped off without harm. The finishing of painted furniture is less critical—only framed panels must be painted before final assembly.

The best part of designing and building your own furniture is making exactly what you need and like. A chair built for your very own body is by far better than one of standard dimensions. Have you ever wondered about that odd corner in your house, the one no standard furniture will fit into? Many outstanding and beautiful pieces have been made for places like this.

Take a piece of cardboard, draw a lifesize piece of furniture on it, and lean it into this corner. If it does not look right, redraw the picture until it does. You will be surprised how much information such an exercise gives you. In case of doubt take a standard design course in your neighborhood art school or college. It will help. Visits to a museum, antique stores, and especially Grandmother's house are very useful.

Above all let me remind you that your ancestors were architects, artists, hunters, potters, farmers, weavers, cooks, preachers, carpenters—you name the rest. If they could do all this, surely you can be a furniture maker.

Glossary

American Lumber Standards: American lumber standards embody provisions for softwood lumber according to recognized classifications, nomenclature, basic grades, sizes, description, measurements, tally, shipping provisions, grade marking, and inspection of lumber. The primary purpose of these standards is to serve as a guide in the preparation or revision of the grading rules of the various lumber manufacturers' associations. A purchaser must, however, make use of association rules, for the basic standards are not in themselves commercial rules.

Annual Growth Ring: The layer of wood growth that develops on a tree during a single growing season.

Benchdogs: Metal or wooden pins, used in conjunction with a vise, to hold work securely for planing, carving, and similar purposes.

Bevel: *See* Chamfer

Butterfly Joint: A flat piece of wood in the shape of two dovetails meeting each other on the narrow end, which is countersunk and glued into adjacent pieces and serves to connect them.

Cambium: A thin layer of tissue between the bark and wood that repeatedly subdivides to form new wood and bark cells.

Centerboard: A board sawed so that the annual rings form an angle of 90 degrees with the wide surface of the piece.

Chamfer: An oblique face formed, usually but not always, at an angle of 45 degrees to the adjacent face.

Chuck: A device for centering and clamping work in a lathe or other tool.

Coated Nail: A nail with a resinous coating to promote friction, therefore increasing the force needed to withdraw it.

Countersink: To cause a head of a screw, bolt, and so on to sink into a prepared depression so as to be flush with, or below, the surface.

Cross-Grain: *See* End Grain.

Dry Rot: A term loosely applied to any dry, crumbly rot but especially to that which, when in an advanced stage, permits the wood to be crushed easily to a dry powder. The term is actually a misnomer for any decay, since all fungi require considerable moisture for growth.

Earlywood: The portion of the annual growth ring that is formed during the early part of the growing season.

End Grain: The grain as seen on a cut made at a right angle to the direction of the fibers (for example, on a cross section of a tree).

Face: The side of the wood that once was facing the center of the tree, when it was still inside the tree.

Frame: A rigid structure formed of relatively slender pieces joined so as to surround and support a panel.

Frame of Table: *See* Skirt.

Glue Joint: A joint secured with the help of an adhesive.

Heartwood: The wood extending from the pith to the sapwood, the cells that no longer participate in the life processes of the tree. Heartwood may contain phenolic compounds, gums, resins, and other materials that usually make it darker and more decay-resistant than sapwood.

Interacting Load Factors: Combined strengths or weaknesses within a construction that influence the whole structure.

Lap Joint: A joint between two members in which an end or section of one, is partly cut away to be overlapped by an end or section of the other, often so that flush surfaces result.

Latewood: The portion of the annual growth ring that is formed after the earlywood formation has ceased. It is usually denser and stronger than earlywood.

Miter: Joint between two pieces of wood meeting at an angle in which each of the butting surfaces is cut to an angle equal to half the angle of junction.

Plain-sawed Wood: Wood that has been sawed parallel to the pith and approximately tangent to the growth rings. Wood is considered plain-sawed when the annual growth rings make an angle of less than 45 degrees with the surface of the piece.

Quarter-sawed Wood: Wood that has been sawed so that the wide surfaces are approximately at right angles to the annual growth rings. Wood is considered quarter-sawed when the rings form an angle of 45 to 90 degrees with the wide surface of the piece.

Rabbet Plane: A plane for cutting recesses in the edge or surface of a board or the like, having a blade set to one side at right angles or diagonally to the direction of the motion.

Rasp: A course file having separate conical teeth.

Right Side of Wood: *See* Face.

Rough-cut: Wood that has not been dressed (surfaced) but that has been sawed, edged, and trimmed.

Sapwood: The wood of pale color near the outside of the log.

Screw Lead: The twisted tip of an auger bit. This tip centers the bit and is of help to pull it into the hole.

Scribe: A pointed instrument used to mark or score wood.

Shim: A thin slip or wedge of wood used to level and fasten work-pieces and other items.

Side Grain: Wood fibers running parallel to the axis of the piece.

Skirt: The framework under the tabletop connecting the legs of the table to each other.

Spline Joint: A joint between two pieces of wood having grooved edges connected by a strip of material fitted into the grooves.

Squared Shank: The upper end of an auger bit squared to provide a better grip for the claws in the chuck of the brace.

Stable Wood: Well-seasoned centerboard or quarter-sawed wood.

Toolsteel: A steel tempered for use in fine tools.

Warp: Any variation from a true or plane surface. Warp includes bow, crook, cup, twist, or any combination thereof.

Wood Fiber: A wood cell from less than $\frac{1}{25}$ to $\frac{1}{3}$ inch long, narrow, tapering, and closed at both ends.

List of sources

TOOLS

It is most unlikely that you will find fine woodworking tools in your neighborhood hardware store. If you let the following mail-order tool suppliers know who and where you are, you will never be without a tool catalog. Often it is less expensive to send for a tool than purchasing it locally.

Brookstone Company
127 Vose Farm Road
Peterborough, N.H. 03458

The Fine Tool Shops, Inc.
20-28 Backus Avenue
Danbury, Conn. 06810

Consumers Bargain Corp.
404 Irvington Street
Pleasantville, N.Y. 10570

Woodcraft Supply Corp.
313 Montvale Avenue
Woburn, Mass. 01888

Frog Tool Co., Ltd.
541 N. Franklin Street
Chicago, Ill. 60610

Wood Is Good Co.
P.O. Box 477
Lakewood, Calif. 90714

Sculpture Associates, Ltd.
114 East 25th Street
New York, N.Y. 10010

Shopsmith Inc.
750 Center Drive
Vandalia, Ohio 45377

WOOD

Wood is best purchased from your neighborhood lumberyard. But if you have no other choice, there are a few mail-order lumber companies willing to serve you. Be aware that if you do not like a material sent to you by mail or freight, the seller is usually willing to exchange it. You pay for transportation, however, which is quite often more expensive than the price of the material itself.

Albert Constantine and Son, Inc.
2050 Eastchester Road
Bronx, N.Y. 10461

Craftsman Wood Service Co.
2727 S. Mary Street
Chicago, Ill. 60608

Educational Lumber Co.
P.O. Box Drawer 5373
Ashville, N.C. 28813

Wicks Organ Company
1100 Fifth Street
Highland, Ill. 62249

The World of Hardwood
P.R.R. Station
Harmans, Md. 21077

Bibliography

All the books available on furniture comprise too long a list to include in this book. Your library will help to serve your needs. After you read a few volumes of furniture history, you may find that the subject is often disassociated from the daily lives of human beings. We are the latest link in a long chain. The form our furniture has taken over the centuries is interwoven with the way we have looked at life and at ourselves. For a look at the chain read:

Clark, Kenneth, *Civilization,* New York: Harper & Row, Pub., 1970.

There are a few other books furniture makers should read. These include:

U.S. Department of Agriculture, *Wood as an Engineering Material.* Forest Products Laboratory, Handbook #72. Washington, D.C.: U.S. Govt. Printing Office, 1974.

Parker, Harry, *Simplified Mechanics and Strength of Materials.* New York: John Wiley, 1961.

And one quarterly magazine every woodworker seems to read, and for good reason, is:

Fine Woodworking Magazine, The Taunton Press, P.O. Box 355, Newtown, Conn. 06470.